Essential Hindi

Written by
Monisha Bhat

Edited by
Laura Riggio

LIVING LANGUAGE®

Published in the United States by Living Language, an imprint of Random House LLC,
a Penguin Random House Company.

www.livinglanguage.com

Editor: Laura Riggio
Production Editor: Ciara Robinson
Production Manager: Tom Marshall
Interior Design: Sophie Chin
Production Design: Ann McBride
Audio Producer: Ok Hee Kolwitz
Typesetting: worldaccent.com

First Edition

ISBN: 978-0-307-97253-8

PRINTED IN THE UNITED STATES OF AMERICA

10 9 8 7 6 5 4 3 2 1

Acknowledgments

Thanks to the Living Language team: Amanda D'Acierno, Dan Zitt, Suzanne McQuade, Erin Quirk, Heather Dalton, Dennis Tyrrell, Fabrizio LaRocca, Siobhan O'Hare, Sophie Chin, Ann McBride, Tina Malaney, Pat Stango, Sue Daulton, Alison Skrabek, Ciara Robinson, Andrea McLin, and Tom Marshall.

How to Use This Course **6**

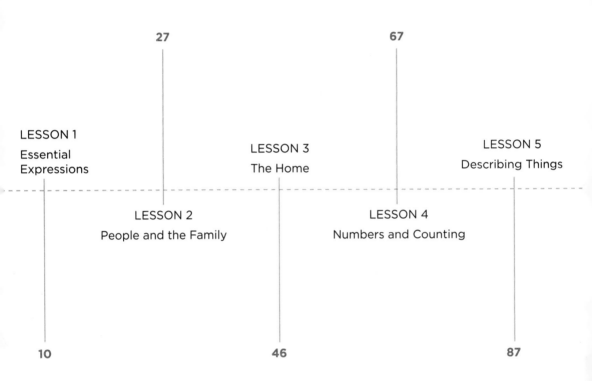

COURSE

OUTLINE

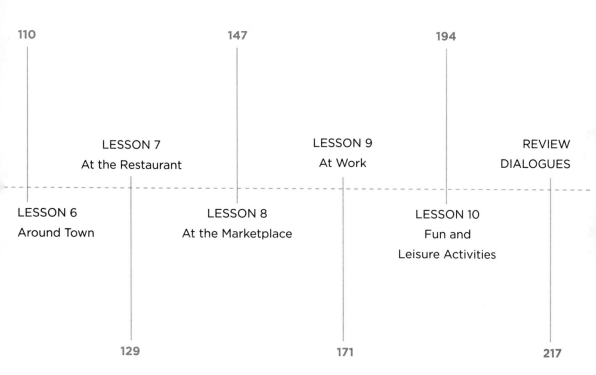

How To Use This Course

नमस्ते!

namaste!

Hello!

Welcome to *Living Language Essential Hindi*! Are you ready to learn how to speak, read, and write Hindi?

Before we begin, let's go over what you'll see in this course. It's very easy to use, but this section will help you get started.

LESSONS

There are 10 lessons in this course. Each lesson is divided into three parts and has the following components:

PART 1

- **Vocabulary Builder 1** listing the key words and phrases for that lesson.
- **Vocabulary Practice 1** to practice what you learned in Vocabulary Builder 1.
- **Grammar Builder 1** to guide you through the structure of the Hindi language (how to form sentences, questions, and so on).

PART 2

- **Vocabulary Builder 2** listing more key words and phrases.
- **Vocabulary Practice 2** to practice what you learned in Vocabulary Builder 2.
- **Grammar Builder 2** for more information on language structure.
- **Work Out 1** for a comprehensive practice of what you've learned so far.

PART 3

- **Bring It All Together** to put what you've learned in a conversational context through a dialogue, monologue, description, or other similar text.
- **Work Out 2** for another helpful practice exercise.
- **Drive It Home** to ingrain an important point of Hindi structure for the long term.
- **Parting Words** outlining what you learned in the lesson.

TAKE IT FURTHER

Take It Further sections are scattered throughout the lesson to provide extra information about the new vocabulary you just saw, expand on grammar points, or introduce additional words and phrases.

WORD RECALL

Word Recall sections appear in-between lessons. They review important vocabulary and grammar from previous lessons, including the one you just finished. These sections will reinforce what you've learned so far in the course, and help you retain the information for the long term.

QUIZZES

This course contains two quizzes: **Quiz 1** is halfway through the course (after Lesson 5), and **Quiz 2** appears after the last lesson (Lesson 10). The quizzes are self-graded so it will be easy for you to test your progress and see if you need to go back and review once again.

REVIEW DIALOGUES

There are five **Review Dialogues** at the end of the course, after Quiz 2. These everyday dialogues review what you learned in Lessons 1–10, introduce new vocabulary and structures, and allow you to become more familiar with conversational Hindi. Each dialogue is followed by comprehension questions that serve as the course's final review.

PROGRESS BAR

You will see a **Progress Bar** on almost every page that has course material. It indicates your current position in the course and lets you know how much progress you've made. Each line in the bar represents a lesson; the final line represents the Review Dialogues.

AUDIO

Look for this symbol ▶ a to help guide you through the audio as you read the book. It will tell you the name of the track to listen to for each section. When you see the symbol, start listening! If you don't see the symbol, then there isn't any audio for that section. The audio can be used on its own—in other words, without the book—when you're on the go. Whether in your car or at the gym, you can listen to the audio to brush up on your pronunciation and review what you've learned in the book.

GUIDE TO READING AND WRITING HINDI

Hindi is written in a script called Devanagari. This beautiful script is actually much easier to learn than you might think, and once you learn it, you can pronounce any Hindi word you see. You will learn how to read and write Devanagari through this book and in the *Guide to Reading and Writing Hindi.*

FREE ONLINE LANGUAGE TOOLS

Go to **www.livinglanguage.com/languagelab** to access your free online Hindi language learning tools. These tools are organized around the lessons in this course and are a fun way to help you to review and practice what you've learned.

Lesson 1: Essential Expressions

पाठ १: आवश्यक अनुसरण

pāṭh ek: āvaśyak anusaraṇ

स्वागत है! **swāgat hai!** *Welcome!* In this first lesson, you'll learn basic courtesy expressions and other useful words and phrases that will help get you started speaking Hindi. You'll learn how to:

- ☐ Greet someone and ask how they're doing.
- ☐ Use short, polite sentences and essential vocabulary to introduce yourself in Hindi.
- ☐ Use the present tense of the verb *to be* with the correct pronouns, which will allow you to make simple sentences in Hindi.
- ☐ Use basic Hindi word order, and begin to read Devanagari.

Look for this symbol ▶ to help guide you through the audio as you're reading the book. It will tell you which track to listen to for each section that has audio. If you don't see the symbol, there isn't any audio for that section. Keep in mind that you can use the audio for practice on the go. Are you ready to begin?

Vocabulary Builder 1

1A Vocabulary Builder 1

नमस्ते	**namaste**	*hello*
नमस्कार	**namaskār**	*goodbye*
धन्यवाद	**dhanyavād**	*thank you*
कोई बात नहीं	**koī bāt nahī̃**	*you're welcome/ it's all right*
अच्छा!	**acchā**	*Okay!/All right!*
अच्छा	**acchā**	*good*
जी	**jī**	*sir/ma'am (affirmative)*
माफ़ कीजिए	**māf kījiye**	*excuse me/sorry*
ठीक	**ṭhīk**	*fine/well*
स्वागत है!	**swāgat hai!**	*Welcome!*
हाँ	**hā̃**	*yes*
नहीं	**nahī̃**	*no*
फिर मिलेंगे।	**phir mileṅge.**	*See you later.*
आप कैसे हैं?	**āp kaise haĩ?**	*How are you? (general)*
आप कैसी हैं?	**āp kaisī haĩ?**	*How are you? (when asking a woman)*

मैं ठीक हूँ।	**maĩ ṭhīk hũ̃.**	*I'm fine.*

Vocabulary Practice 1

Let's practice the vocabulary that you've learned. Match the Hindi in the first column to the English equivalent in the second.

1. ठीक **ṭhīk**	a. *How are you?*
2. धन्यवाद। **dhanyavād.**	b. *sir/ma'am (affirmative)*
3. कोई बात नहीं। **koi baat nahī̃.**	c. *You're welcome.*
4. जी **jī**	d. *Thank you.*
5. माफ़ कीजिये। **māf kījiye.**	e. *no*
6. नहीं **nahī̃**	f. *fine/good*
7. आप कैसे हैं? **āp kaise haĩ?**	g. *Excuse me.*

ANSWER KEY

1. f; 2. d; 3. c; 4. b; 5. g; 6. e; 7. a

Grammar Builder 1

1B Grammar Builder 1

Let's review the vocabulary you've learned so far.

नमस्कार	**namaskār**	*hello*
धन्यवाद!	**dhanyavād**	*Thank you!*
कोई बात नहीं	**koī bāt nahī̃**	*you're welcome/ it's all right*
स्वागत है!	**swāgat hai!**	*Welcome!*
फिर मिलेंगे	**phir mileṅge**	*see you later*
जी	**jī**	*sir/ma'am (affirmative)*
माफ़ कीजिये	**māf kījiye**	*excuse me/sorry*

PERSONAL PRONOUNS

Personal pronouns are used in place of nouns. In Hindi, the personal pronouns are:

मैं	**maĩ**	*I*
तुम	**tum**	*you*
वह	**vah/vo***	*she/he/it/that*

यह	yah/ye*	*she/he/it/this*
हम	hum	*we*
आप	āp	*you*
वे	ve	*they/those*
ये	ye	*they/these*

*Please note the two pronunciations of वह and यह: vah and vo, and yah and ye. The latter two pronunciations are more modern and what you will hear in everyday speech in India.

As you can see above, there are two ways of saying *you* in Hindi: आप āp and तुम tum. These forms can be used when addressing one person or more than one person, and they are both polite forms. There is also another singular personal pronoun for *you*: तू tū. This, however, is an extremely informal manner of addressing someone; it is used to address someone younger, or very close. As someone just learning Hindi, you should stick to using आप āp or तुम tum.

Take It Further 1

As you make your way through Essential Hindi, we'll gradually introduce you to Devanagari, the writing system used for Hindi. At this point, turn to your *Guide to Reading and Writing Hindi*, and cover:

- ☐ Devanagari and Hindi Pronunciation
- ☐ Group 1: Vowels

Vocabulary Builder 2

1C Vocabulary Builder 2

आपका नाम क्या है?	**āpkā nām kyā hai?**	*What's your name?*
मेरा नाम रीमा है।	**merā nām rīmā hai.**	*My name's Reema.*
मैं दिल्ली से हूँ।	**maĩ dillī se hū̃.**	*I'm from Delhi.*
क्या हाल है?	**kyā hāl hai?**	*How's it going? (informal)*
आपसे मिलकर ख़ुशी हुई।	**āpse milkar khuśī huī.**	*Pleasure meeting you.*
मुझे भी।	**mujhe bhī.**	*Same here. (lit.: me too)*
और आप?	**aur āp?**	*And you?*
रीया प्रोफेसर है।	**riyā profesar hai.**	*Ria is a professor.*

Take It Further 2

1D Take It Further 2

Did you notice the possessive pronoun मेरा **merā** in मेरा नाम रीमा है **merā nām rīmā hai** *My name is Reema*? Also notice the ending का **kā** attached to the pronoun आप **āp** (*you*), which produces आपका **āpkā** (*your*). का **kā** is called a postposition, because it's a particle that comes after a noun or pronoun, just as a preposition in English comes before. Hindi has many important postpositions that you'll learn gradually. For now, it will help to remember these two possessives:

मेरा	**merā**	*mine, my*
आपका	**āpkā**	*yours, your*

Vocabulary Practice 2

Translate the following into Hindi.

1. *How's it going?*

2. *My name is Reema.*

3. *I'm fine, thank you.*

4. *I am from Delhi.*

5. *Excuse me, what is your name?*

6. *You're welcome. See you later.*

7. *Pleasure meeting you.*

ANSWER KEY

1. क्या हाल है? **kyā hāl hai?** 2. मेरा नाम रीमा है। **merā nām rīmā hai.** 3. मैं ठीक हूँ, धन्यवाद। **maĩ ṭhīk hũ, dhanyavād.** 4. मैं दिल्ली से हूँ। **maĩ dillī se hũ.** 5. माफ़ कीजिये, आपका नाम क्या है? **māf kījiye, āpkā nām kyā hai?** 6. कोई बात नहीं, फिर मिलेंगे। **koi baat nahĩ. phir mileṅge.** 7. आपसे मिलकर ख़ुशी हुई। **āpse milkar khuśī huī.**

Grammar Builder 2

1E Grammar Builder 2

PRESENT TENSE OF THE VERB *TO BE*

Have you noticed the extensive use of है **hai** so far? This is a form of the verb होना **honā** (*to be*). Let's look at the full conjugation of होना **honā** with the pronouns you've already seen.

मैं हूँ	**maĩ hũ**	*I am*
तुम हो	**tum ho**	*you are*
वह है	**vah/vo hai**	*she/he/it/that is*
यह है	**yah/ye hai**	*she/he/it/this is*
हम हैं	**hum haĩ**	*we are*
आप हैं	**āp haĩ**	*you are*
वे हैं	**ve haĩ**	*they/those are*
ये हैं	**ye haĩ**	*they/these are*

Work Out 1

1F Work Out 1

Let's go over everything that you've learned so far. Listen to your audio and fill in the blanks with the words that you hear. For additional audio-only practice, listen to the English phrases and translate them into Hindi.

1. ___________ **rāju hai**

   ___________ राजू है।

   That is Raju.

2. **namaste,** ___________ **kaise haĩ?**

   नमस्ते, ___________ कैसे हैं?

   Hello, how are you?

3. ___________ **dillī se hū̃**

   ___________ दिल्ली से हूँ।

   I am from Delhi.

4. **maĩ ṭhīk** ___________**, dhanyavād.**

   मैं ठीक ___________, धन्यवाद।

   I am fine, thank you.

5. ___________ **profesar haĩ.**

   ___________ प्रोफेसर हैं।

   They are professors.

6. **tum kaise** ___________**?**

   तुम कैसे ___________?

   How are you?

7. ye kyā ___________?
यह क्या ___________?
What is this?

ANSWER KEY

1. vah वह 2. āp आप 3. maĩ मैं 4. hū̃ हूँ 5. ve वे 6. ho हो 7. hai है

Bring It All Together

1G Bring It All Together

Now let's listen to a short conversation between Jay and his teacher Maya, who are meeting after a long time. Maya also asks about Madan, a mutual friend.

जय: नमस्कार माया जी। आप कैसी हैं?
jay: namaskār māyā jī. āp kaisī haĩ?
Jay: Hello, Maya (lit.: Maya Ma'am). How are you?

माया: नमस्कार जय। मैं अच्छी हूँ। और तुम?
māyā: namaskār jay. maĩ acchī hū̃. aur tum?
Maya: Hello Jay. I'm well. And you?

जय: मैं ठीक हूँ।
jay: maĩ ṭhīk hū̃.
Jay: I am fine.

माया: मदन कैसा है? वह कहाँ है आजकल?
māyā: madan kaisā hai? vah kahā̃ hai ājkal?
Maya: How is Madan? Where is he these days?

जय: मदन अच्छा है। वह दिल्ली में है।
jay: **madan acchā hai. vah dilli meĩ hai.**
Jay: *Madan is good. He is in Delhi.*

माया: अरे वाह, अच्छा है।
māyā: **are vāh, acchā hai.**
Maya: *Oh, nice. That's good.*

जय: आपसे मिलकर ख़ुशी हुई।
jay: **āpse milkar khuśī huī.**
Jay: *Pleasure meeting you.*

माया: मुझे भी।
māyā: **mujhe bhī.**
Maya: *Me too.*

जय: अच्छा, फिर मिलेंगे, नमस्कार!
jay: **acchā, phir mileṅge, namaskār!**
Jay: *Okay, see you later, bye!*

माया: ठीक है, नमस्कार।
māyā: **ṭhīk hai, namaskār.**
Maya: *Okay, bye.*

Take It Further 3

1H Take It Further 3

Did you notice these few new terms?

कहाँ?	**kahā̃**	*Where?*
आजकल	**ājkal**	*these days*
अरे वाह!	**are vāh**	*Oh, nice!*

Did you also notice the sounds ū̃, ā̃, and ĩ in:

हूँ	**hū̃**	*am*
हाँ	**hā̃**	*yes*
हैं	**haĩ**	*are*

These are nasalized vowels. Any vowel, with the exception of ṛ in Hindi, can be nasalized. That means that a good part of the airflow passes through the nose. You may not realize it, but English has plenty of nasal vowels. Any time a vowel comes before *–m*, *–n*, or *–ng* in the same syllable, it's nasalized. Say *dope* and *don't*, and pay close attention to the vowel. It's nasalized in *don't*. In Hindi, a nasal vowel is marked by a kind of half-moon on its side with a dot over it, placed above the vowel. If part of the vowel itself is written above the headstroke, then just the dot is used. Notice that in transliteration, nasalization is marked by the tilde:

कूँ	**kū̃**
काँ	**kā̃**
कों	**kō̃**

Now let's take a very quick look at the word order in Hindi. You may have noticed that it is different from the word order used in English. Let's look at some of these differences: First, the verb *to be*, in its various forms, comes at the end of a sentence.

मैं अच्छी हूँ!	**maĩ acchī hū̃!**	*I am fine!*
आप कैसे हैं?	**āp kaise haĩ?**	*How are you?*

Second, interrogatives usually come before the verb. But the interrogative क्या **kyā** (*what*) comes at the beginning of a yes/no question.

आपका नाम क्या है?	**āpkā nām kyā hai?**	*What is your name?*
क्या तुम मदन हो?	**kyā tum madan ho?**	*Are you Madan?*
क्या आप राज हैं?	**kyā āp rāj haĩ?**	*Are you Raj?*

Work Out 2

Now let's practice what you've learned so far. Fill in the blanks with the missing words.

1. *Excuse me, what is your name?*

   माफ़ कीजिए, आप का __________ क्या है?

   māf kījiye, āpkā __________ kyā hai?

2. *My name is Ria.*

   __________ नाम रिरी है।

   __________ nām Riyā hai.

3. *They are professors.*

   __________ प्रोफेसर हैं।

   __________ profesar haĩ.

4. *We are from Pune.*

   __________ पुणे से हैं।

   __________ puṇe se haĩ.

5. *Yes, this is Jay.*

   हाँ, __________ जय है।

   hā̃, __________ jay hai.

6. *Okay, goodbye. See you later.*

   अच्छा, ____________________। फिर मिलेंगे।

   acchā, ____________________. phir mileṅge.

7. *Are you from Delhi?*

क्या ________ दिल्ली से हैं?

kyā ________ dillī se haĩ?

ANSWER KEY

1. नाम **nām** 2. मेरा **merā** 3. वह **vah** 4. हम **ham** 5. यह **yah** 6. नमस्कार **namaskār** 7. आप **āp**

Drive It Home

In each lesson, you'll see a Drive It Home exercise. These exercises may seem repetitive, and even simple, but they're designed to make the Hindi that you've learned more automatic, so it moves from your short term memory to your long term memory. Don't skip these exercises, no matter how easy they may seem. As you learn more Hindi grammar, you'll see that the repetition is very helpful for your retention!

For now, let's practice personal pronouns, and the verb होना **honā** (*to be*).

A. Translate the following pronouns into Hindi:

1. *I* ________

2. *she* ________

3. *they* ________

4. *this* ________

5. *we* ________

6. *you* ________

B. Now give the appropriate form of होना **honā** for each personal pronoun below.

1. वे **ve** ____________

2. तुम **tum** ____________

3. मैं **maĩ** ____________

4. ये **ye** ____________

5. वह **vah** ____________

6. आप **āp** ____________

ANSWER KEY

A. 1. मैं **maĩ** 2. वह **vah** 3. वे **ve** 4. यह **yah** 5. हम **ham** 6. आप **āp**/तुम **tum**

B. 1. हैं **haĩ** 2. हो **ho** 3. हूँ **hũ** 4. है **hai** 5. है **hai** 6. हैं **haĩ**

Parting Words

बधाई! **badhāī!** *Congratulations!* You've come to the end of your first lesson! By now you should know how to:

- ☐ Greet someone and ask how they're doing. (Still unsure? Go back to Vocabulary Builder 1.)
- ☐ Use short, polite sentences and essential vocabulary to introduce yourself in Hindi. (Still unsure? Go back to Grammar Builder 1.)
- ☐ Use the present tense of the verb *to be* with the correct pronouns, which will allow you to make simple sentences in Hindi. (Still unsure? Go back to Grammar Builder 2.)
- ☐ Use basic Hindi word order, and begin to read Devanagari. (Still unsure? Go back to Take It Further 3 .)

Word Recall

Let's review the most important vocabulary you learned in Lesson 1. Match the two columns.

1. धन्यवाद।
   dhanyavād.
2. आपका नाम क्या है?
   āpkā nām kyā hai?
3. माफ़ कीजिए।
   māf kījiye.
4. फिर मिलेंगे।
   phir mileṅge.
5. आप कैसे हैं?
   āp kaise haĩ?
6. आपसे मिलकर ख़ुशी।
   āpse milkar khuśī huī.
7. मेरा नाम रीमा है।
   merā nām rīmā hai.
8. मैं ठीक हूँ।
   maĩ ṭhīk hū̃.

a. *What is your name?*

b. *See you later.*

c. *My name is Rima*

d. *How are you?*

e. *Pleasure meeting you.*

f. *Excuse me*

g. *Thank you.*

h. *I am fine.*

ANSWER KEY

1. g; 2. a; 3. f; 4. b; 5. d; 6. e; 7. c; 8. h

Lesson 2: People and Family

पाठ २: लोग और परिवार

pāṭh do: log aur parivār

नमस्ते! **namaste!** *Hello!* This second lesson is all about people and the family. You'll learn how to:

- □ Talk about different family members.
- □ Express possession with words like *my* and *your.*
- □ Express possession with the equivalent of *have.*
- □ Put it all together in a conversation about the family.

Are you ready to begin?

Vocabulary Builder 1

2A Vocabulary Builder 1

परिवार	**parivār**	*family (m.)*
आदमी	**ādmi**	*man (m.)*
औरत	**aurat**	*woman (f.)*
माँ/माता	**mā̃/mātā**	*mother (f.)*

पिता	**pitā**	*father (m.)*
भाई	**bhāī**	*brother (m.)*
बहन	**bahan**	*sister (f.)*
दादा	**dādā**	*paternal grandfather (m.)*
नाना	**nānā**	*maternal grandfather (m.)*
दादी	**dādī**	*paternal grandmother (f.)*
नानी	**nānī**	*maternal grandmother (f.)*
बेटी	**beṭī**	*daughter (f.)*
लड़की	**laṛkī**	*girl (f.)*
लड़का	**laṛkā**	*boy (m.)*
बेटा	**beṭā**	*son (m.)*

Vocabulary Practice 1

Let's practice the vocabulary that you've learned. Match the Hindi in the first column to the English equivalent in the second.

1. औरत
aurat

a. paternal grandfather

2. बेटा

beṭā

3. पिता

pitā

4. दादा

dādā

5. नानी

nānī

6. बहन

bahan

7. भाई

bhaī

b. sister

c. woman

d. maternal grandmother

e. son

f. brother

g. father

ANSWER KEY

1. c; 2. e; 3. g; 4. a; 5. d; 6. b; 7. f

Take it Further 1

2B Take It Further 1

Though there are two terms for mother—माँ/माता **mā̃/mātā**—we'll use the more common, and spoken form माँ **mā̃** here in this lesson.

Do you remember the affirmative जी **jī** that you learned in Lesson 1? In Hindi, it is often used when talking to elders in the family:

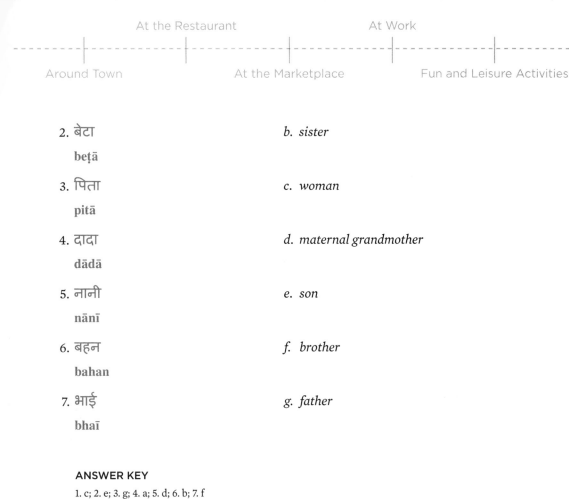

पिताजी	pitājī	*father*
चाचाजी	cācājī	*uncle*
माताजी	mātājī	*mother*
नानीजी	nānījī	*maternal grandmother*

Grammar Builder 1

2C Grammar Builder 1

INTRODUCTION TO GENDER

Hindi is a language with grammatical gender. That means that every noun, even ones referring to inanimate objects, is either masculine or feminine. So far you've mostly learned nouns that refer to people, and in these cases grammatical gender typically matches natural gender. And you'll notice from the examples above and words in Vocabulary Builder 1 that most of the feminine nouns end in the vowel ī ई:

MASCULINE	FEMININE
दादा dādā *paternal grandfather*	दादी dādī *paternal grandmother*

लड़का **laṛkā** *boy*	लड़की **laṛkī** *girl*
नाना **nānā** *maternal grandfather*	नानी **nānī** *maternal grandmother*
बेटा **beṭā** *son*	बेटी **beṭī** *daughter*

But there are exceptions:

भाई **bhāī** *brother*	बहन **bahan** *sister*
आदमी **ādmi** *man*	औरत **aurat** *woman*
पिता **pitā** *father*	माँ/माता **mā̃/mātā** *mother*

It is a good idea to memorize the gender of each new noun that you learn, because in Hindi, many grammatical details depend on gender. One of those details is possessives like *my* and *your*, which we'll look at right now.

Singular Possessives

Do you remember the two possessives you learned in the last lesson?

मेरा	**merā**	*my*
मेरा नाम रीमा है।	**merā nām rīmā hai.**	*My name is Reema.*
आपका	**apkā**	*your*
आपका नाम क्या है?	**āpkā nām kyā hai?**	*What's your name?*

मेरा **merā** (*my*) and आपका **āpkā** (*your*) are masculine forms, because they describe or refer to the masculine noun नाम **nām** (*name*). It does not matter whether the speaker of the sentence is a man or a woman. On the other hand, if the sentences were about a feminine noun, for example बहन **bahan** (*sister*), the forms would be मेरी **merī** and आपकी **āpkī**.

Let's look at the singular possessives now, in both their masculine and feminine forms. Note that they can be translated as adjectives (*my, your*) or pronouns (*mine, yours*).

MASCULINE	FEMININE	MEANING
मेरा **merā**	मेरी **merī**	*my/mine*
तुम्हारा **tumhārā**	तुम्हारी **tumhārī**	*your/yours*
आपका **āpkā**	आपकी **āpkī**	*your/yours*
उसका **uskā**	उसकी **uskī**	*her/hers/his*
इसका **iskā**	इसकी **iskī**	*her/hers/his*

Let's look at the possessives to describe family relations:

मेरा भाई	**merā bhāī**	*my brother*
मेरी माँ	**merī mā̃**	*my mother*
मेरी बहन	**merī bahan**	*my sister*
तुम्हारी बेटी	**tumhārī beṭī**	*your daughter*
आपकी दादी	**āpkī dādī**	*your grandma*
तुम्हारा भाई	**tumhārā bhāī**	*your brother*

आपका लड़का	**āpkā laṛkā**	*your boy*
उसका पिता	**uskā pitā**	*his/her father*
इसका बेटा	**iskā beṭā**	*his/her son*
उसकी माँ	**uskī mā̃**	*his/her mother*
इसकी बेटी	**iskī beṭī**	*his/her daughter*

Take It Further 2

Let's take a closer look at Devanagari now. Turn to the *Guide to Reading and Writing Hindi* and cover:

☐ Group 2 Consonants: क **ka**, ख **kha**, ग **ga**, and घ **gha**

Vocabulary Builder 2

▶ 2D Vocabulary Builder 2

पति	**pati**	*husband (m.)*
पत्नी	**patnī**	*wife (f.)*
मौसी	**mausī**	*aunt (mother's sister) (f.)*
मामा	**māmā**	*uncle (mother's brother) (m.)*

चाचा	cācā	*uncle (father's brother) (m.)*
बुआ	buā	*aunt (father's sister) (f.)*
बड़ा	baṛā	*elder/older/large (m.)*
बड़ी	baṛī	*elder/older/large (f.)*
छोटा	choṭā	*younger/small (m.)*
छोटी	choṭī	*younger/small (f.)*
कौन	kaun	*who*
कोई	koī	*someone*

Vocabulary Practice 2

Match the English expressions on the left with the Hindi equivalents on the right.

1. *large family*
2. *younger brother*
3. *uncle (maternal)*

a. कौन
kaun

b. बड़ी बहन
baṛī bahan

c. मामा
māmā

4. *who*

d. माँ
mā̃

5. *father's sister*

e. बड़ा परिवार
baṛā parivār

6. *older sister*

f. बुआ
buā

7. *mother*

g. छोटा भाई
choṭā bhāī

ANSWER KEY

1. e; 2 g; 3. c; 4. a; 5. f; 6. b; 7. d

Grammar Builder 2

2E Grammar Builder 2

EXPRESSING *HAVE*

In Hindi, there isn't an equivalent of the verb *to have*. A variety of different constructions are used instead. To express *have* with family members, the possessives that you learned earlier in the lesson are used along with the verb *to be*, होना **honā**, and a term to quantify the possession. For now, we'll restrict ourselves to singular possession. As we go ahead, you will gradually learn about plural, as well as inanimate possession, which takes a different construction from human possession. Note that the gender of the family member that you *have* determines the gender of the possessive.

मेरा एक चाचा है।	**merā ek cācā hai.**	*I have one uncle on my father's side.*
मेरी एक नानी है।	**merī ek nānī hai.**	*I have a grandmother.*
उसका एक मामा है।	**uskā ek māmā hai.**	*She has a maternal uncle.*
वह उसकी बेटी है।	**vah uskī beṭī hai.**	*That is his daughter.*
यह मेरा मामा है।	**yah merā māmā hai.**	*This is my maternal uncle.*

Take it Further 3

2F Take It Further 3

As you may have noticed, Hindi does not have articles (*the* or *a/an*), so the noun परिवार **parivār** can be translated as *family*, *a family*, or *the family*, depending on context. But the number एक **ek** (*one*) can be used in a way similar to the indefinite article *a/an*, especially for stress or emphasis.

वह वकील है।	**vah vakīl hai**	*He's a lawyer.*
वह एक वकील है।	**vah ek vakīl hai**	*He is a lawyer. (not a doctor or an engineer, etc.)*

Work Out 1

2G Work Out 1

Let's review what we've learned so far. Listen to your audio, and fill in the missing words. Then translate the sentences.

1. **merā ____________ baṛā hai.**
   मेरा ____________ बड़ा है।

2. **tum merī ____________ ho.**
   तुम मेरी ____________ हो।

3. **merī ____________ vakīl hai.**
   मेरी ____________ वकील है।

4. **yah uskā ____________ hai.**
   यह उसका ____________ है।

5. **vah merī ____________ hai.**
   वह मेरी ____________ है।

6. **merī ek ____________ hai.**
   मेरी एक ____________ है

7. **vah uskā ____________ hai.**
   वह उसका ____________ है।

ANSWER KEY

1. **parivār** परिवार (*My family is big.*) 2. **bahan** बहन (*You are my sister.*) 3. **beṭī** बेटी (*My daughter is a lawyer.*) 4. **beṭā** बेटा (*This is her son.*) 5. **nānī** नानी (*She is my maternal grandmother.*) 6. **bahan** बहन (*I have a sister.*) 7. **bhāī** भाई (*That is her brother.*)

Bring It All Together

2H Bring It All Together

Now let's listen in as Raj and Anita look at the family album. Raj is pointing out different people in the pictures to Anita, a young and curious relative who is visiting him.

राज: यह मेरा पिता है और वह मेरी माँ है।
raj: yah merā pitā hai aur vahmerī mā̃ hai.
Raj: This is my father and that is my mother.

अनीता: क्या यह लड़का आपका बेटा है?
anitā: kyā yah laṛkā āpkā beṭā hai?
Anita: Is this boy your son?

राज: नहीं. वह मेरा छोटा भाई है। वह दिल्ली में है।
raj: nahī̃. vah merā choṭā bhāī hai. vah dillī mẽ hai.
Raj: No. That is my younger brother. He is in Delhi.

अनीता: अच्छा! मेरी नानी भी दिल्ली में हैं।
anitā: acchā! merī nānī bhī dillī mẽ haĩ.
Anita: Okay! My grandmother is also in Delhi.

राज: हाँ। यह तुम्हारी माँ है। वह औरत तुम्हारी मौसी है।
raj: hā̃. yah tumhārī mā̃ hai. vah aurat tumhārī mausī hai.
Raj: Yes. This is your mother. That woman is your aunt.

अनीता: यह औरत कौन है?
anitā: yah aurat kaun hai?
Anita: Who is this woman?

राज: यह मेरा पत्नी है और यह मेरा छोटा बेटा है। मेरी एक बड़ी बेटी भी है।
raj: **yah merā patnī hai aur yah merā choṭā beṭā hai. merī ek baṛī beṭī bhī hai.**
Raj: *This is my wife and my younger son. I also have an older daughter.*

अनीता: यह औरत कौन है?
anitā: **yah aurat kaun hai?**
Anita: *Who is this woman?*

राज: वह मेरी बुआ सीमा है। उसका एक बेटा है और एक बेटी। यह उसकी बेटी है।
raj: **vah merī buā sīmā hai. uskā ek beṭā hai aur ek beṭī. yah uskī beṭī hai.**
Raj: *That is my aunt, my father's sister, Seema. She has a son and a daughter. This is her daughter.*

अनीता: आपका परिवार बड़ा है!
anitā: **āpkā parivār baṛā hai!**
Anita: *Your family is big!*

Take it Further 4

21 Take It Further 4

Both forms of *you*, आप **āp** and तुम **tum** are polite. However, आप **āp** is commonly used by younger people when addressing someone older or in a position of authority. So, when Saroj talks to Anita, who is younger, she can choose to say तुम्हारा **tumhārā** (*your/yours*), while Anita uses आपका **āpkā**. In certain households आप **āp** is the norm, irrespective of the age or authority of the person being addressed.

Did you notice these few new terms?

भी	**bhī**	*also/too*
और	**aur**	*and*

Work Out 2

Let us now practice what you've learned so far. Fill in the blanks with the missing words.

1. *I have a sister. She is small.*

   मेरी एक ________________ है। वह छोटी है।

   merī ek ________________ hai. vah choṭī hai.

2. *That is your uncle (maternal).*

   वह तुम्हारा ________________ है।

   vah tumhārā ________________ hai.

3. *My elder brother is Ram.*

   मेरा ________________ राम है।

   merā ________________ rām hai.

4. *My family is large.*

   मेरा ________________ बड़ा है।

   merā ________________ baṛā hai.

5. *Is she your older girl?*

क्या वह तुम्हारी बड़ी ________________ है?

kyā vah tumhārī baṛī ________________ hai?

6. *Seema is my younger paternal aunt.*

सीमा मेरी ________________ है।

sīmā merī ________________ hai.

7. *That is my paternal grandfather.*

वह मेरा ________________ है।

vah merā ________________ hai.

ANSWER KEY

1. बहन **bahan** 2. मामा **māmā** 3. बड़ा भाई **baṛā bhāī** 4. परिवार **parivār** 5. लड़की **laṛkī** 6. छोटी बुआ **choṭī buā** 7. दादा **dādā**

Drive It Home

A. Translate each phrase into Hindi using the appropriate possessive.

1. *my family* ________________

2. *her uncle* ________________

3. *his brother* ________________

4. *her aunt (father's sister)* ________________

5. *your (formal) elder sister* ________________

6. *my uncle (father's brother)* ________________

B. Match the two columns:

1. *This is my maternal grandmother.*	a. वह मेरा चाचा है। **vah merā cācā hai.**
2. *That is my uncle (paternal).*	b. यह तुम्हारी माँ है। **yah tumhārī mā̃ hai.**
3. *Your younger brother.*	c. इसका पिता। **iskā pita.**
4. *This is your mother.*	d. तुम्हारा छोटा भाई। **tumhārā choṭā bhāī.**
5. *his/her/this one's father*	e. यह आदमी कौन है? **yah ādmī kaun hai?**
6. *Who is this man?*	f. उसकी बड़ी बेटी। **uskī baṛī beṭī.**
7. *His older daughter.*	g. यह मेरी नानी है। **yah merī nānī hai.**

ANSWER KEY

A. 1. मेरा परिवार **merā parivār** 2. उसका चाचा **uskā cācā** 3. उसका भाई **uskā bhāī** 4. उसकी बुआ **uskī buā** 5. आपकी बड़ी बहन **āpkī baṛī bahan** 6. मेरा चाचा **merā cācā**

B. 1. g; 2. a; 3. d; 4. b; 5. c; 6. e; 7. f

Culture Note

Indian families often have two or more generations living together in the same house. The system is traditionally patriarchal, with the women leaving their parental homes to settle in with their husband's parents and siblings. In such joint families, it is common to have married brothers living in the same house they grew up in, with their wives and children and parents.

Joint families are more common in rural areas where farming is a major occupation. It is also common among families who own businesses in big cities where members of even the third generation live and work together with their grandparents who likely founded the business.

If adult children move to another city or town for higher education and work, they may choose to live and raise a family there. Even then, for many Indians, vacations and holidays still mean getting together with the extended family in their home town and spending time with relatives.

Parting Words

You've come to the end of your second lesson! By now you should know how to:

- ☐ Talk about different family members. (Still unsure? Go back to Vocabulary Builder 1.)
- ☐ Express possession with words like *my* and *your.* (Still unsure?Go back to Grammar Builder 1.)
- ☐ Express possession with the equivalent of *have.* (Still unsure? Go back to Grammar Builder 2.)
- ☐ Put it all together in a conversation about the family. (Still unsure? Go back to Bring It All Together.)

Word Recall

Let's review the vocabulary together with correct possessives. Match the two columns.

1. लड़का
   laṛkā
2. मेरा पति
   merā patī
3. उसका मामा
   uskā māmā
4. मेरी पत्नी
   merī patnī
5. उसका भाई
   uskā bhāī
6. वह आदमी
   vah ādmī
7. मेरी बुआ
   merī buā

a. *her maternal uncle*
b. *boy*
c. *my paternal aunt*
d. *my husband*
e. *that man*
f. *my wife*
g. *his brother*

ANSWER KEY

1. b; 2. d; 3. a; 4. f; 5 g; 6. e; 7. c

Lesson 3: The Home

पाठ ३: घर

pāṭh tīn: ghar

In this lesson, you'll learn basic expressions and other useful words and phrases that will help get you started speaking around the house.

In this lesson, you will learn:

- ☐ Vocabulary for around the home.
- ☐ Gender (inanimate) and some basic plurals.
- ☐ Some more possessives.
- ☐ Devanagari: Group 3 Consonants: च **ca**, छ **cha**, ज **ja**, झ **jha**.

Are you ready to begin?

Vocabulary Builder 1

3A Vocabulary Builder 1

घर	**ghar**	*house (m.)*
कमरा	**kamrā**	*room (m.)*
बाथरूम	**bāthrūm**	*bathroom/restroom (m.)*

गुसलखाना	**gusalkhānā**	*bathroom/restroom (m.)*
खिड़की	**khiṛkī**	*window (f.)*
दरवाज़ा	**darvāzā**	*door (m.)*
रसोई	**rasoī**	*kitchen (f.)*
बैठक	**baithak**	*living room (f.)*
सोने का कमरा	**sone kā kamrā**	*bedroom (m.)*
बालकनी	**bālkanī**	*balcony (f.)*
दीवार	**dīvār**	*wall (f.)*
पंखा	**pankhā**	*fan (m.)*
किताब	**kitāb**	*book (f.)*
परदा	**pardā**	*curtain (m.)*

Vocabulary Practice 1

Let's practice the vocabulary that you've learned. Match the Hindi expressions in the first column to their English equivalent in the second.

1. रसोई
   rasoī

a. *door*

2. घर
ghar

b. *window*

3. कमरा
kamrā

c. *house*

4. बैठक
baithak

d. *kitchen*

5. गुसलखाना
gusalkhānā

e. *room*

6. खिड़की
khiṛkī

f. *bathroom*

7. दरवाज़ा
darvāzā

g. *living room*

ANSWER KEY

1. d; 2. c; 3. e; 4. g; 5. f; 6. b; 7. a

Grammar Builder 1

3B Grammar Builder 1

PLURALS

You're already familiar with singular nouns from Lesson 2. Now let's look at how to form plural nouns. In Hindi, plural endings depend on the gender of the noun (remember that words ending in आ ā are generally masculine, while those ending in ई ī are generally feminine). Here are some general rules that will help you form the plural.

Masculine nouns ending with आ ā usually take on the ending ए e.

कमरा **kamrā** *room*	कमरे **kamre** *rooms*
दरवाज़ा **darvāzā** *door*	दरवाज़े **darvāze** *doors*
पंखा **pankhā** *fan*	पंखे **pankhe** *fans*

Some masculine nouns ending with a consonant may not change.

घर **ghar** *home*	घर **ghar** *homes*
मकान **makān** *house*	मकान **makān** *houses*

Some masculine nouns take the ending एं ẽ.

दीवार **dīvār** *wall*	दीवारें **dīwārẽ** *walls*
किताब **kitāb** *book*	किताबें **kitābẽ** *books*

Feminine nouns ending with ई **ī** usually take the ending इयाँ **iyā̃**.

खिड़की **khiṛkī** *window*	खिड़कियाँ **khiṛkiyā̃** *windows*
कुर्सी **kursī** *chair*	कुर्सियाँ **kursiyā̃** *chairs*

You'll learn more about numbers and plurals in Lesson 4, but keep these general rules in mind when you are forming plurals.

Take It Further 1

Let's look at the Devanagari now. Turn to the *Guide to Reading and Writing Hindi*, and cover:

- ☐ Group 3 Consonants च ca, छ cha, ज ja, झ jha

Vocabulary Builder 2

3C Vocabulary Builder 2

अलमारी	**almārī**	*cupboard (f.)*
टीवी	**tīvī**	*television (f.)*
सामान	**sāmān**	*stuff/belongings (m.)*
पलंग	**palang**	*bed (m.)*
बरतन	**bartan**	*utensil (m.)*
कुर्सी	**kursī**	*chair (f.)*
हवादार	**havādār**	*airy/well-ventilated*
यह किसका घर है?	**yah kiskā ghar hai?**	*Whose house is this?*
आप किधर रहते हैं?	**āp kidhar rahate haĩ?**	*Where do you stay/live?*
यह मेरा घर है।	**yah merā ghar hai.**	*This is my home.*

Take It Further 2

3D Take It Further 2

You just learned how to say, *Where do you stay/live?* आप किधर रहते हैं? **āp kidhar rahate haĩ?** This is an example of the present imperfective tense, which is used in Hindi to express a habitual or general action, similar to the English simple present *I go* or *she speaks.* When you form the present imperfective, you need two elements: first, a form of the main verb (in this case, *to live/stay* रहना **rahanā**) and the conjugated form of the verb *to be,* होना **honā**. In Lesson 1 you learned how to conjugate the verb होना **honā**. You use a form of the verb *to live/stay,* रहना **rahanā**, that is technically called the imperfective participle, but don't worry about the label! All you need to know is that it's like an adjective and it changes form depending upon the gender and number of the subject. You will learn more about using verbs as we go along, but for now, let's look at the forms of the imperfective participle रहना **rahanā**.

M. SINGULAR	M. PLURAL	F. SINGULAR	F. PLURAL
रहता **rahatā**	रहते **rahate**	रहती **rahatī**	रहती **rahatī**

Now let's look at रहना **rahanā** together with the subject pronouns and the different forms of *to be,* होना **honā**. Note that the pronoun is followed by the imperfective participle of रहना **rahanā** followed by the conjugated form of होना **honā**.

MASCULINE	FEMININE
मैं रहता हूँ **maĩ rahatā hũ** *I stay*	मैं रहती हूँ **maĩ rahatī hũ** *I stay*
तुम रहते हो **tum rahate ho** *you stay*	तुम रहती हो **tum rahatī ho** *you stay*
आप रहते हैं **āp rahate haĩ** *you stay*	आप रहती हैं **āp rahatī haĩ** *you stay*
हम रहते हैं **ham rahate haĩ** *we stay*	हम रहती हैं **ham rahatī haĩ** *we stay*
वह/यह रहता है **vah/yah rahatā hai** *he stays*	वह/यह रहती है **vah/yah rahatī hai** *she stays*
वे/ये रहते हैं **ve/ye rahate haĩ** *they stay*	वे/ये रहती हैं **ve/ye rahatī haĩ** *they stay*

✎ Vocabulary Practice 2

Match the English expressions on the left with the Hindi equivalents on the right:

1. *wall*	a. सोने का कमरा **sone kā kamrā**
2. *bedroom*	b. यह मेरा घर है **yah merā ghar hai**
3. *kitchen*	c. दीवार **dīvār**
4. *door*	d. खिड़की **khiṛkī**
5. *window*	e. आप किधर रहते हैं? **āp kidhar rahate haĩ?**
6. *Where do you stay?*	f. दरवाज़ा **darvāzā**
7. *this is my home*	g. रसोई **rasoī**

ANSWER KEY

1. c; 2. a; 3. g; 4. f; 5. d; 6. e; 7. b

Grammar Builder 2

3E Grammar Builder 2

POSSESSION

In Lesson 2, you learned how to say *my*, *your*, *his*, and *her* with singular possessions:

मेरी कुर्सी	**merī kursī**	*my chair*
तुम्हारा पलंग	**tumhārā palang**	*your bed*

Now let's look at the same possessives with plural possessions. Remember that Hindi possession depends on the gender and number of the object being possessed.

M. PLURAL	F. PLURAL	MEANING
मेरे **mere**	मेरी **merī**	*my/mine*
तुम्हारे **tumhāre**	तुम्हारी **tumhārī**	*your/yours*
आपके **āpke**	आपकी **āpkī**	*your/yours*
उसके **uske**	उसकी **uskī**	*her/hers; his; of that*

इसके **iske**	इसकी **iskī**	*her/hers; his; of this*

Examples:

मेरे भाई	**mere bhāī**	*my brothers*
मेरी किताबें	**merī kitābẽ**	*my books*
उसके बेटे	**uske bete**	*her sons*
तुम्हारी कुर्सियां	**tumharī kursiyā̃**	*your chairs*
उसकी किताबें	**uskī kitābẽ**	*his books*

Let's now look at plural possessors, corresponding to the English *our/ours, your/yours (pl.)*, and *their/theirs*. Just like the singular possessives, *our, your (pl.)*, and *their* have different endings depending on the gender and number of the possession. First let's look at the form you use with singular possessions.

M. PLURAL	F. PLURAL	MEANING
हमारा **hamārā**	हमारी **hamārī**	*our/ours*
इनका **inkā**	इनकी **inkī**	*their/theirs/of these*

उनका **unkā**	उनकी **unkī**	*their/theirs/of those*

Examples:

हमारा घर	**hamārā ghar**	*our house*
उनकी कुर्सी	**unkī kursī**	*their chair*
उनका भाई	**unkā bhāī**	*their brother*
हमारी बहन	**hamārī bahan**	*our sister*

Let's now look at the forms you use with plural possessions.

M. PLURAL	F. PLURAL	MEANING
हमारे **hamāre**	हमारी **hamārī**	*our/ours*
उनके **unke**	उनकी **unkī**	*their/theirs/of those*
इनके **inke**	इनकी **inkī**	*their/theirs/of these*

Examples:

हमारे घर	**hamāre ghar**	*our houses*
उनकी कुर्सियां	**unkī kursiyā̃**	*their chairs*
उनके भाई	**unke bhāī**	*their sisters*
हमारे भाई	**hamāre bhāī**	*our brothers*

Work Out 1

3F Work Out 1

Listen to your audio and fill in the blanks with the words that you hear. Then translate each sentence.

1. यह ____________________ बैठक है।

   yah ____________________ baithak hai.

2. ये ____________________ कमरे हैं।

   ye ____________________ kamrẽ haĩ.

3. यह उसका ____________________ है।

   yah uskā ____________________ hai.

4. वे उसकी ____________________ हैं।

   ve uskī ____________________ haĩ.

5. ये उनके ____________________ हैं।

   ye unke ____________________ haĩ.

6. यह ____________ उसका है।

yah ____________ uskā hai.

7. वह बालकनी ____________ है।

vah balkanī ____________ hai.

ANSWER KEY

1. हमारे **hamāre** (*This is our living room.*) 2. मेरे **mere** (*These are my rooms.*) 3. पलंग **palang** (*This bed is hers.*) 4. कुर्सियाँ **kursiyā̃** (*Those are her chairs.*) 5. मकान **makān** (*These are their houses.*) 6. सामान **sāmān** (*This stuff is hers.*) 7. उनकी **unkī** (*That is their balcony.*)

Bring It All Together

3G Bring It All Together

Now let's listen as Raj describes his home.

आपका स्वागत है! यह हमारा घर है।
āpkā swāgat hai! yah hamarā ghar hai.
Welcome! This is our home.

यह बैठक है, वे सोने के कमरे हैं, और वह रसोई है।
yah baithak hai, ve sone ke kamre haĩ, aur vah rasoī hai.
This is the living room, those are the bedrooms, and that is the kitchen.

बहुत सी खिड़कियाँ और एक बालकनी भी है।
bahut sī khiṛkiyā̃ aur ek bālkanī bhī hai.
There are many windows and a balcony as well.

मेरा एक बेटा है और एक बेटी। एक कमरा उनका है।
merā ek beṭā hai aur ek beṭī. ek kamrā unkā hai.
I have a son and a daughter. One room is theirs.

एक कमरा मेरा और मेरी पत्नी सीमा का है।
ek kamrā mera aur merī patnī sīma kā hai.
One room is for me and my wife Seema.

मेरा एक छोटा चचेरा भाई है, अमित। एक कमरा उसका है।
merā ek choṭa cacerā bhāī hai, Amit. ek kamrā uskā hai.
I have a younger cousin (paternal uncle's son), Amit. One room is his.

सभी कमरे हवादार हैं।
sabhī kamrẽ havādār haĩ.
All rooms are airy.

Take it Further 3

3H Take It Further 3

You'll learn about adjectives in greater detail in Lesson 5, but did you notice these new words?

बहुत सी	**bahut sī**	*several, many*
बहुत सी खिड़कियाँ	**bahut sī khiṛkiyā̃**	*several windows*

You also saw a new term for cousin, चचेरा भाई **cacerā bhāī**. In Hindi, there is no single term for cousin. Instead, they're known by the way in which they are related.

चचेरा भाई	**cacerā bhāī**	*paternal uncle's son (cousin brother)*
ममेरा भाई	**mamerā bhāī**	*maternal uncle's son (cousin brother)*
चचेरी बहन	**cacerī bahan**	*paternal uncle's daughter (cousin sister)*
ममेरी बहन	**mamerī bahan**	*maternal uncle's daughter (cousin sister)*
मौसेरी बहन	**mauserī bahan**	*maternal aunt's daughter (cousin sister)*
मौसेरा भाई	**mauserā bhāī**	*maternal aunt's son (cousin brother)*
बुआ की बेटी	**buā ki beṭī**	*paternal aunt's daughter (cousin sister)*
बुआ का बेटा	**buā kā beṭā**	*paternal aunt's son (cousin brother)*

Work Out 2

Let's practice what you've learned. Fill in the blanks with the missing words.

1. यह ________________ घर है।

   yah ________________ ghar hai.

   This is my house.

2. वे ________________ परदे हैं।

ve ________________ parde haĩ.

Those are your curtains.

3. वह ________________ खिड़की है।

vah ________________ khiṛkī hai.

That is her window.

4. यह ________________ है और वह बालकनी है।

yah ________________ hai, aur vah bālkanī hai.

This is the kitchen and that is the balcony.

5. यह तुम्हारा ________________ है।

yah tumhārā ________________ hai.

This is your stuff.

6. ________________ किधर है?

________________ kidhar hai?

Where is the bathroom?

7. ये ________________ उसके हैं।

ye ________________ uske haĩ.

These are her rooms.

ANSWER KEY

1. मेरा merā 2. तुम्हारे tumhāre 3. उसकी uskī 4. रसोई rasoī 5. सामान sāmān 6. गुसलखाना gusalkhānā
7. कमरे kamre

Drive It Home

A. Provide the correct plural forms in Hindi:

1. *home* ________________

2. *window* ________________

3. *door* ________________

4. *curtain* ________________

5. *house* ________________

B. Fill in the blanks with the appropriate possessive form:

1. ये ________________ बरतन हैं।

   ye ________________ bartan haĩ.

   These are their utensils.

2. वे ________________ किताबें हैं।

   ve ________________ kitābe haĩ.

   Those are my books.

3. यह ________________ अलमारी है।

   yah ________________ almārī hai.

   This is your cupboard.

4. यह ________________ सामान है।

   yah ________________ sāmān hai.

   This is her stuff.

5. ये ____________ परदे हैं।

ye ____________ parde haĩ.

These are her curtains.

ANSWER KEY

A. 1. घर ghar 2. खिड़कियाँ khiṛkiyā̃ 3. दरवाज़े darvāze 4. परदे parde 5. मकान makān

B. 1. उनके unke 2. मेरी merī 3. तुम्हारी tumhārī 4. उसका uskā 5. उसके uske

Culture Note

In most Indian homes, space is shared; siblings share a room, closet space, and belongings like books and clothes. Parents have a room to themselves, but even this room is never out-of-bounds for other family members. This is especially true in a city like Mumbai where houses are often built small and compact. If there are grandparents living in, the younger children in the family will often share space and a lot of time with them in activities such as eating, studying, and sleeping with them. Often, the grandparents will play the role of informal baby-sitters, thus helping the mother to go out and work.

A typical Indian house has bedrooms, a living room, and a kitchen. Bathrooms are shared by the family. There may be balconies that are used for ventilation or as utility areas for washing up, etc. Some households also have a room set aside for guests or relatives.

Parting Words

You've come to the end of your third lesson! By now you should know:

☐ Vocabulary for around the home. (Still unsure? Go back to Vocabulary Builder 1.)

- ☐ Gender (inanimate) and some basic plurals. (Still unsure? Go back to Grammar Builder 1.)
- ☐ Some more possessives. (Still unsure? Go back to Grammar Builder 2.)
- ☐ Devanagari: Group 3 alphabets: च **ca**, छ **cha**, ज **ja**, झ **jha**. (Still unsure? Go back to Take It Further 1.)

Word Recall

Let's review the most important vocabulary you learned. Match the two columns:

1. *house*	a. किताब **kitāb**
2. *living room*	b. बालकनी **bālkanī**
3. *balcony*	c. दरवाज़ा **darvāzā**
4. *kitchen*	d. बैठक **baiṭhak**
5. *utensils*	e. दीवार **dīvār**
6. *books*	f. घर **ghar**
7. *walls*	g. रसोई **rasoī**
8. *door*	h. बरतन **bartan**

ANSWER KEY

1. f; 2. d; 3. b; 4. g ; 5. h ; 6. a ; 7. e; 8. c

Lesson 4: Numbers and Counting

पाठ ४: अंक तथा गिनती

pāth cār: ãnk tathā gintī

In this lesson, you'll learn how to count in Hindi. You'll learn:

- ☐ Numbers 1 through 100.
- ☐ More about forming plurals.
- ☐ Devanagari: Group 4 Consonants: त **ta**, थ **tha**, द **da**, ध **dha**.

Vocabulary Builder 1

4A Vocabulary Builder 1

एक १	**ek**	*one 1*
दो २	**do**	*two 2*
तीन ३	**tīn**	*three 3*
चार ४	**cār**	*four 4*
पांच ५	**pā̃c**	*five 5*
छह ६	**chah**	*six 6*
सात ७	**sāt**	*seven 7*

आठ ८	āṭh	*eight 8*
नौ ९	nau	*nine 9*
दस १०	das	*ten 10*
कितने?	kitne?	*How many?*
गिनती	gintī	*count*
साल	sāl	*years*
लोग	log	*people*

Vocabulary Practice 1

Let's practice the vocabulary that you've learned. Match the Hindi in the first column to the English equivalent in the second.

1. नौ
   nau
2. आठ
   āṭh
3. सात
   sāt
4. तीन
   tīn

a. *four*
b. *nine*
c. *eight*
d. *six*

5. छह
chah

e. *two*

6. दो
do

f. *seven*

7. चार
cār

g. *three*

ANSWER KEY

1. b; 2. c; 3. f; 4. g; 5. d; 6. e; 7. a

Take it Further 1

Let's focus on Devanagari now. Turn to the *Guide to Reading and Writing Hindi* and cover:

☐ Group 4 Consonants: त **ta**, थ **tha**, द **da**, ध **dha**

Grammar Builder 1

▶ 4B Grammar Builder 1

MORE PLURALS

You learned about gender and plurals in the previous lessons. Now that you've learned how to count to ten, let's practice forming plurals in Hindi. Remember that the endings for plural nouns vary depending on the gender of that noun. Let's review.

MASCULINE SINGULAR ENDING IN आ ā	PLURAL WILL END IN ए e
लड़का **laṛkā** *boy*	लड़के **laṛke** *boys*
बेटा **beṭā** *son*	बेटे **beṭe** *sons*

MASCULINE SINGULAR ENDING IN CONSONANT	PLURAL ENDING REMAINS SAME
घर **ghar** *home*	घर **ghar** *homes*
शहर **śahar** *city*	शहर **śahar** *cities*

There are some masculine words that end in ई ī and आ ā, and whose plural forms remain the same.

भाई **bhāī** *brother*	भाई **bhāī** *brothers*
चाचा **cācā** *paternal uncle*	चाचा **cācā** *paternal uncles*
आदमी **ādmī** *man*	आदमी **ādmī** *men*
मामा **māmā** *maternal uncle*	मामा **māmā** *maternal uncles*

FEMININE SINGULAR ENDING IN ई ī	PLURAL WILL END IN इयाँ iyā̃
लड़की **laṛkī** *girl*	लड़कियाँ **laṛkiyā̃** *girls*
बेटी **beṭī** *daughter*	बेटियाँ **beṭiyā̃** *daughters*

FEMININE SINGULAR ENDING IN CONSONANT	PLURAL ENDING WILL TAKE THE VOWEL एं ẽ
औरत **aurat** *woman*	औरतें **auratẽ** *women*
किताब **kitāb** *book*	किताबें **kitābẽ** *books*

Let's make a few sentences using plurals you just learned.

ये मेरे मामा हैं।	**ye mere māmā haĩ.**	*These are my uncles.*
वे मेरी बहनें हैं।	**vah meribahanẽ haĩ.**	*Those are my sisters.*
वे मेरे भाई हैं।	**ve mere bhāī haĩ.**	*They are my brothers.*
वे दस किताबें हैं।	**ve das kitābẽ haĩ.**	*Those are ten books.*
ये चार शहर हैं।	**ye cār śahar haĩ.**	*These are four cities.*

Remember that when talking about plurals, the verb is nasalized:

SINGULAR	PLURAL
वह मेरा भाई है।	वे मेरे भाई हैं।
vah merā bhāī hai.	**ve mere bhāī haĩ.**
That's my brother.	*Those are my brothers.*

Take It Further 2

4C Take It Further 2

Let's take a look at the plurals of some new nouns now:

बच्चा **baccā** *child*	बच्चे **bacce** *children*
भतीजी **bhatījī** *niece*	भतीजियाँ **bhatījiyā̃** *nieces*
भतीजा **bhatījā** *nephew*	भतीजे **bhatīje** *nephews*
दोस्त **dost** *friend*	दोस्त **dost** *friends*

Vocabulary Builder 2

4D Vocabulary Builder 2

ग्यारह ११	**gyārah**	*eleven 11*
बारह १२	**bārah**	*twelve 12*
तेरह १३	**terah**	*thirteen 13*
चौदह १४	**caudah**	*fourteen 14*
पंद्रह १५	**pandrah**	*fifteen 15*
सोलह १६	**solah**	*sixteen 16*
सत्रह १७	**satrah**	*seventeen 17*
अठारह १८	**aṭhārah**	*eighteen 18*
उन्नीस १९	**unnīs**	*nineteen 19*
बीस २०	**bīs**	*twenty 20*

Vocabulary Practice 2

Let's practice the terms you've learned so far. Match the Hindi numbers in the first column with the English numbers in the second.

1. उन्नीस
   unnīs

a. *twelve*

2. सोलह
solah

3. बीस
bīs

4. बारह
bārah

5. चौदह
caudah

6. तेरह
terah

7. अठारह
aṭhārah

b. *eighteen*

c. *fourteen*

d. *twenty*

e. *sixteen*

f. *nineteen*

g. *thirteen*

ANSWER KEY

1. f; 2. e; 3. d; 4. a; 5. c; 6. g; 7. b

Grammar Builder 2

4E Grammar Builder 2

THE HINDI COUNTING SYSTEM

Hindi has a unique system of numbers. You've already learned numbers 1–20, which have to be memorized. But after 20, Hindi numbers follow a different logic from the "20 and 1 is 21" system you might expect. After 20, numbers are made of prefixes attached to the number in the tens place. For example, the +1 prefix is इक– **ik–**:

इक्कीस	२१	**ikkīs**	*21*
इकतीस	३१	**ikattīs**	*31*

The +2 prefix is बा– **ba–**:

बाईस	२२	**bāīs**	*22*
बावन	५२	**bāvan**	*52*

Here is a list of 21–100. Notice the patterns.

इक्कीस २१ **ikkīs** *twenty-one* *21*	बाईस २२ **bāīs** *twenty-two* *22*	तेईस २३ **teīs** *twenty-three* *23*	चौबीस २४ **caubīs** *twenty-four* *24*	पच्चीस २५ **pacīs** *twenty-five* *25*
छब्बीस २६ **chabbīs** *twenty-six* *26*	सत्ताईस २७ **satāīs** *twenty-seven* *27*	अठाईस २८ **aṭhāīs** *twenty-eight* *28*	उनतीस २९ **unnatīs** *twenty-nine* *29*	तीस ३० **tīs** *thirty* *30*
इकतीस ३१ **ikattīs** *thirty-one* *31*	बत्तीस ३२ **battīs** *thirty-two* *32*	तैंतीस ३३ **taiñtīs** *thirty-three* *33*	चौंतीस ३४ **cauñtīs** *thirty-four* *34*	पैंतीस ३५ **paiñtīs** *thirty-five* *35*

छत्तीस ३६ **chattīs** *thirty-six* *36*	सैंतीस ३७ **saiñtīs** *thirty-seven* *37*	अड़तीस ३८ **aḍatīs** *thirty-eight* *38*	उनतालीस ३९ **untālīs** *thirty-nine* *39*	चालीस ४० **cālīs** *forty* *40*
इकतालीस ४१ **ikatālīs** *forty-one* *41*	बयालीस ४२ **bāyālīs** *forty-two* *42*	तैंतालीस ४३ **taiñtālīs** *forty-three* *43*	चौंतालीस ४४ **cauñtālīs** *forty-four* *44*	पैंतालीस ४५ **paiñtālīs** *forty-five* *45*
छियालीस ४६ **chhiyālīs** *forty-six* *46*	सैंतालीस ४७ **saiñtālīs** *forty-seven* *47*	अड़तालीस ४८ **aḍatālīs** *forty-eight* *48*	उनचास ४९ **uncās** *forty-nine* *49*	पचास ५० **pacās** *fifty* *50*
इक्यावन ५१ **ikyāvan** *fifty-one* *51*	बावन ५२ **bāvan** *fifty-two* *52*	तिरेपन ५३ **tirepan** *fifty-three* *53*	चौवन ५४ **cauvan** *fifty-four* *54*	पचपन ५५ **pacapan** *fifty-five* *55*
छप्पन ५६ **chappan** *fifty-six* *56*	सत्तावन ५७ **sattāvan** *fifty-seven* *57*	अट्ठावन ५८ **aṭṭhāvan** *fifty-eight* *58*	उनसठ ५९ **unasaṭh** *fifty-nine* *59*	साठ ६० **sāṭh** *sixty* *60*

इकसठ ६१ **ikasaṭh** *sixty-one* *61*	बासठ ६२ **bāsaṭh** *sixty-two* *62*	तिरेसठ ६३ **tiresaṭh** *sixty-three* *63*	चौंसठ ६४ **cauñsaṭh** *sixty-four* *64*	पैंसठ ६५ **paiñsaṭh** *sixty-five* *65*
छियासठ ६६ **chiyāsaṭh** *sixty-six* *66*	सड़सठ ६७ **saṛsaṭh** *sixty-seven* *67*	अड़सठ ६८ **aṛsaṭh** *sixty-eight* *68*	उनहत्तर ६९ **unahattar** *sixty-nine* *69*	सत्तर ७० **sattar** *seventy* *70*
इकहत्तर ७१ **ikahattar** *seventy-one* *71*	बहत्तर ७२ **bahattar** *seventy-two* *72*	तिहत्तर ७३ **tihattar** *seventy-three* *73*	चौहत्तर ७४ **cauhattar** *seventy-four* *74*	पचहत्तर ७५ **pacahattar** *seventy-five* *75*
छिहत्तर ७६ **chihattar** *seventy-six* *76*	सतहत्तर ७७ **satahattar** *seventy-seven* *77*	अठहत्तर ७८ **aṭhahattar** *seventy-eight* *78*	उनासी ७९ **unāsī** *seventy-nine* *79*	अस्सी ८० **assī** *eighty* *80*
इक्यासी ८१ **ikyāsī** *eighty-one* *81*	बयासी ८२ **bayāsī** *eighty-two* *82*	तिरासी ८३ **tirāsī** *eighty-three* *83*	चौरासी ८४ **caurāsī** *eighty-four* *84*	पचासी ८५ **pacāsī** *eighty-five* *85*

छियासी ८६ **chiyāsī** *eighty-six* *86*	सतासी ८७ **satāsī** *eighty-seven* *87*	अठासी ८८ **aṭhāsī** *eighty-eight* *88*	नवासी ८९ **navāsī** *eighty-nine* *89*	नब्बे ९० **nabbe** *ninety* *90*
इक्यानवे ९१ **ikyānave** *ninety-one* *91*	बानवे ९२ **bānave** *ninety-two* *92*	तिरानवे ९३ **tirānave** *ninety-three* *93*	चौरानवे ९४ **caurānave** *ninety-four* *94*	पचानवे ९५ **pacānave** *ninety-five* *95*
छियानवे ९६ **chiyānave** *ninety-six* *96*	सत्तानवे ९७ **sattānave** *ninety-seven* *97*	अट्ठानवे ९८ **aṭṭhānave** *ninety-eight* *98*	निन्यानवे ९९ **ninyānave** *ninety-nine* *99*	एक सौ १०० **ek sau** *one hundred* *100*

Work Out 1

4F Work Out 1

Listen to your audio and fill in the blanks with the words that you hear.

1. ये ________________ कमरे हैं।

   ye ________________ kamre haĩ.

2. वे ________________ परदे हैं।

   ve ________________ parde haĩ.

3. वह ________________ साल की है।

   vah ________________ sāl kī hai.

4. उसके परिवार में ____________ लोग हैं।

Uske parivār mẽ ____________ log haĩ.

5. मेरे भाई के पास ____________ किताबें हैं।

mere bhaī ke pās ____________ kitābẽ haĩ.

6. वे ____________ घर हैं।

ve ____________ ghar haĩ.

7. यह ____________ बालकनी है।

yah ____________ bālkanī hai.

ANSWER KEY

1. दस **das** (*These are ten rooms.*) 2 साठ **sāṭh** (*Those are sixty curtains.*) 3. पैंतालीस **paĩtālīs** (*She is forty-five years old.*) 4. तीन **tīn** (*Her family has three members.*) 5. बाईस **bāīs** (*My brother has twenty two books.*) 6. पांच **pā̃c** (*There are five houses.*) 7. एक **ek** (*This is one balcony.*)

Bring It All Together

4G Bring It All Together

Now let's listen to a description of a large family that lives together.

हमारा परिवार बड़ा है। मेरे ३ चाचा हैं और २ बुआ हैं।

hamārā parivār barā hai. mere tīn cācā haĩ aur do buā haĩ.

Our family is large. I have three paternal uncles and two paternal aunts.

हमारे घर में १८ कमरे हैं।

hamāre ghar mẽ aṭhārah kamre haĩ.

There are eighteen rooms in our home.

सबके २-२ कमरे हैं। एक रसोई है।
sabke do-do kamre haĩ. ek rasoī hai.
Everyone has two rooms each. There is one kitchen.

एक कमरे में १०० किताबें हैं।
ek kamre mẽ sau kitābẽ haĩ.
One room has one hundred books.

हमारे ३० पेड़ हैं और ५० छोटे पौधे हैं।
hamāre tīs peṛ haĩ aur pacās choṭe paudhe haĩ.
We have thirty trees and fifty small plants.

हमारे ७ पालतू कुत्ते और ४ बिल्लियाँ भी हैं।
hamāre sāt pāltu kutte aur cār billīyā̃ bhī haĩ.
We also have seven pet dogs and four cats.

Take It Further 3

4H Take It Further 3

Did you notice some new terms?

पालतू	**pāltu**	*domesticated (pets)*
में	**mẽ**	*in*
सबके	**sabke**	*of everyone*
कुत्ते	**kutte**	*dogs*
बिल्लियाँ	**billīyā̃**	*cats*

पेड़	**peṛ**	*trees*
पौधे	**paudhe**	*plants*

Work Out 2

Let's practice what you've learned. Fill in the blanks with the missing words.

1. उसकी ________________ हैं।

   uskī ________________ haĩ.

   She has seventeen books.

2. हमारे घर में ________________ कमरे हैं।

   hamāre ghar mẽ ________________ kamre haĩ.

   Our house has twenty bedrooms.

3. यह ________________ बच्चा है और वे ________________ बच्चे हैं।

   yah ________________ baccā hai aur ve ________________ bacce haĩ.

   This is one child and those are nine children.

4. ________________ कुर्सियां हैं?

   ________________ kursiyā̃ haĩ?

   How many chairs are there?

5. हमारे ________________ पेड़ हैं।

   Hamāre ________________ peṛ haĩ.

   We have twenty-two trees.

6. मेरी ________ बहने हैं और ________ भाई हैं।

Merī ________ bahanẽ haĩ aur ________ bhāī haĩ.

I have three sisters and two brothers.

7. उनकी ________ खिड़कियाँ हैं।

unkī ________ khiṛkiyā̃ haĩ.

They have thirty-two windows.

ANSWER KEY

1. सत्रह **satrah** 2. बीस **bīs** 3. एक **ek**, नौ **nau** 4. कितनी **kitnī** 5. बाईस **bāīs** 6. तीन **tīn**, दो **do** 7. बत्तीस **battīs**

Drive It Home

Translate the following into Hindi.

1. *How many are those?*

____

2. *These are ten.*

____

3. *I have three brothers.*

____

4. *My home has two bedrooms.*

____

5. *This room has four windows.*

____

6. *I have two sisters.*

7. *My family has six members.*

ANSWER KEY

1. वे कितने हैं? ve kitne hai? 2. ये दस हैं। ye das haĩ. 3. मेरे तीन भाई हैं। mere tīn bhāī haĩ. 4. मेरे घर में दो सोने के कमरे हैं। mere ghar mẽ do sone ke kamre haĩ. 5. इस कमरे में चार खिड़कियाँ हैं। is kamre mẽ chār khiṛkiyā̃ haĩ. 6. मेरी दो बहने हैं। mere do bahane haĩ. 7. मेरे परिवार में छह लोग हैं। mere parivār mẽ chah log haĩ.

Take It Further 4

41 Take It Further 4

When counting beyond 100 in Hindi, you have to take the word for *hundred*, सौ sau, and add the relevant number to it.

एक सौ एक	ek sau ek	*101*
एक सौ इक्कीस	ek sau ikkīs	*121*
एक सौ पचास	ek sau pacās	*150*
दो सौ	do sau	*200*
दो सौ बत्तीस	do sau battīs	*232*
तीन सौ	tīn sau	*300*

This pattern continues up to 999. Beyond 999, a new word is introduced: एक हज़ार **ek hazār** (*one thousand*).

Parting Words

You've come to the end of your lesson! By now you should know:

- ☐ Numbers 1 through 100. (Still unsure? Go back to Grammar Builder 2.)
- ☐ More about forming plurals. (Still unsure? Go back to Grammar Builder 1.)
- ☐ Devanagari: Group 4 Consonants: त **ta**, थ **tha**, द **da**, ध **dha**. (Still unsure? Go back to Take It Further 1.)

Word Recall

Match the Hindi in the first column with its English equivalents in the right.

1. बारह
   bārah
2. दस
   das
3. सोलह
   solah
4. आठ
   āṭh
5. तीन
   tīn
6. सात
   sāt
7. इक्कीस
   ikkīs

a. *eight*
b. *twenty one*
c. *twelve*
d. *three*
e. *ten*
f. *sixteen*
g. *seven*

ANSWER KEY

1. c; 2. e; 3. f; 4. a; 5. d; 6. g; 7. b

Lesson 5: Describing Things

पाठ ५: वर्णन

pāṭh pā̃c: varṇan

In this lesson, you'll learn basic expressions and other useful words and phrases that will help get you begin to describe people and things. You'll learn:

- ☐ Basic adjectives to describe people and objects, both animate and inanimate.
- ☐ Adjective agreement with singular and plural nouns.
- ☐ Devanagari: Group 5 consonants: Retroflex consonants: ट ṭa, ठ ṭha, ड ḍa, ढ ḍha.

Are you ready to begin?

Vocabulary Builder 1

5A Vocabulary Builder 1

बड़ा	**baṛā**	*big*
छोटा	**choṭā**	*small*
अच्छा	**acchā**	*good*
बुरा	**burā**	*bad*
गरम	**garam**	*hot*

ठंडा	**ṭhanḍā**	*cold*
लम्बा	**lambā**	*tall*
छोटा	**choṭā**	*short*
मोटा	**moṭā**	*fat*
पतला	**patlā**	*thin*
कैसा?	**kaisā?**	*how?*
ऊँचा	**ū̃cā**	*high*
नीचा	**nīcā**	*low*
पुराना	**purānā**	*old*
नया	**nayā**	*new*
सुन्दर	**sundar**	*beautiful*

Vocabulary Practice 1

Let's practice the vocabulary that you've learned. Match the Hindi in the first column to the English equivalent in the second.

1. नया
nayā

a. *big*

2. ठंडा
ṭhanḍā
b. *cold*

3. ऊँचा
ū̃cā
c. *high*

4. बुरा
burā
d. *new*

5. बड़ा
baṛā
e. *tall*

6. लम्बा
lambā
f. *small*

7. छोटा
choṭā
g. *bad*

ANSWER KEY

1. d; 2. b; 3. c; 4. g; 5. a; 6. e; 7. f

Take It Further 1

5B Take it Further 1

Let's look at the Devanagari now. Turn to the *Guide to Reading and Writing Hindi*, and cover:

☐ Group 5 Consonants: Retroflex consonants ट ṭa, ठ ṭha, ड ḍa, ढ ḍha

Grammar Builder 1

5B Grammar Builder 1

ADJECTIVE AGREEMENT WITH SINGULAR NOUNS

Let's look at how to use the adjectives you saw in Vocabulary 1. In Hindi, there are two kinds of adjectives, variable and invariable.

Variable adjectives must agree with the gender and number of the noun they're referring to, while invariable ones do not change. However, it is very easy to differentiate between the two.

Variable adjectives take the ending आ ā in masculine singular form, while the invariable adjectives are the ones ending in consonants. Don't worry if you do not recognize some of the words, you will get to see them more often throughout this course.

VARIABLE ADJECTIVES	INVARIABLE ADJECTIVES
बड़ा **baṛā** *big*	सुन्दर **sundar** *beautiful*
ठंडा **ṭhanḍā** *cold*	नरम **naram** *soft*

ऊँचा ū̃cā *high*	लाल lāl *red*
बुरा burā *bad*	बहुत bahut *a lot/many*

The general rules that apply to gender in Hindi also apply to adjective agreement. That is, most masculine forms end in आ ā, while the feminine forms end in ई ī. Take a look at the two forms of the adjectives below. Note that those forms which change according to gender are variable adjectives, while those that remain constant are invariable adjectives.

MASCULINE (SINGULAR)	FEMININE (SINGULAR)	
नया nayā	नई nayī	*new*
ठंडा ṭhaṇḍā	ठंडी ṭhaṇḍī	*cold*
ऊँचा ū̃cā	ऊँची ū̃cī	*high*
बुरा burā	बुरी burī	*bad*

बड़ा **baṛā**	बड़ी **baṛī**	*big*
लम्बा **lambā**	लम्बी **lambī**	*tall*
छोटा **choṭā**	छोटी **choṭī**	*small*
सुन्दर **sundar**	सुन्दर **sundar**	*beautiful*
बहुत **bahut**	बहुत **bahut**	*a lot/many*

Let's look at some examples. Notice how variable adjectives like मोटा **moṭā** (*fat*) and अच्छा **acchā** (*good*) change form according to the gender of the noun.

राम (*m.*) **rām** *Ram*	राम मोटा है। **rām moṭā hai.**	*Ram is fat.*
घर (*m.*) **ghar** *house*	आपका घर अच्छा है। **āpkā ghar acchā hai.**	*Your house is good.*

औरत (*f.*) **aurat** *woman*	वह औरत मोटी है। **vah aurat moṭī hai.**	*That woman is fat.*
शहर (*m.*) **śahar** *city*	वह सुन्दर शहर है। **vah sundar śahar hai.**	*That is a beautiful city.*
औरत (*f.*) **aurat** *woman*	वह सुन्दर औरत है। **vah sundar aurat hai.**	*That is a beautiful woman. (She is a beautiful woman.)*

Here are more examples.

ठंडा पानी	**ṭhandā pānī**	*cold water*
बुरी किताब	**burī kitāb**	*bad book*
छोटा भाई	**choṭā bhāī**	*small brother*
ऊंची दीवार	**ū̃cī dīvār**	*high wall*

Vocabulary Builder 2

5C Vocabulary Builder 2

पीला	**pīlā**	*yellow (m.)*

लाल	**lāl**	*red (m.)*
हरा	**harā**	*green (m.)*
नीला	**nīlā**	*blue (m.)*
काला	**kālā**	*black (m.)*
सफ़ेद	**safed**	*white*
गरम	**garam**	*hot*
कैसा है?	**kaisā hai?**	*how is . . . ? (m.)*
कैसी है?	**kaisī hai?**	*how is . . . ? (f.)*
रंग	**rang**	*color (m.)*

Take it Further 2

5D Take It Further 2

Most of the terms for colors and other adjectives that end in the sound आ **ā** are masculine. Their endings change to ई **ī** when describing a feminine noun. Let's look at a few examples using feminine nouns like कुर्सी **kursī** (*chair*), दीवार **dīvār** (*wall*), and खिड़की **khiṛkī** (*window*).

पीली कुर्सी	**pīlī kursī**	*yellow chair*
हरी दीवार	**harī dīvār**	*green wall*

काली कुर्सी	**kālī kursī**	*black chair*
नीली खिड़की	**nīlī khiṛkī**	*blue window*

Vocabulary Practice 2

Match the English expressions on the left with the Hindi equivalents on the right.

1. *white* — a. कैसी है? **kaisī hai?**
2. *how is . . . ? (f.)* — b. पीला **pīlā**
3. *blue* — c. सफ़ेद **safed**
4. *hot* — d. हरा **harā**
5. *green* — e. लाल **lāl**
6. *red* — f. गरम **garam**
7. *yellow* — g. नीला **nīlā**

ANSWER KEY

1. c; 2. a; 3. g; 4. f; 5. d; 6. e; 7. b

Grammar Builder 2

5E Grammar Builder 2

ADJECTIVE AGREEMENT WITH PLURAL NOUNS

You know that variable adjectives change form depending on the gender and number of the noun they're describing. In Grammar Builder 1, we looked at singular forms. Now, let's look at plural forms.

M. PLURAL	F. PLURAL	
नए **naye**	नई **nayī**	*new*
ठंडे **ṭhaṇḍe**	ठंडी **ṭhaṇḍī**	*cold*
ऊंचे **ūnce**	ऊँची **ū̃cī**	*high*
बुरे **bure**	बुरी **burī**	*bad*
बड़े **baṛe**	बड़ी **baṛī**	*big*

लम्बे **lambe**	लम्बी **lambī**	*tall*
छोटे **choṭe**	छोटी **choṭī**	*small*
पीले **pīle**	पीली **pīlī**	*yellow*
हरे **hare**	हरी **harī**	*green*
काले **kāle**	काली **kālī**	*black*
नीले **nīle**	नीली **nīlī**	*blue*

Let's look at some example sentence using these adjectives. Remember that invariable adjectives will not change their original form, regardless of the gender or number of the noun they're describing.

MASCULINE	FEMININE
मेरे सुन्दर परदे **mere sundar parde** *my beautiful curtains*	मेरी नई किताबें **merī nayī kitābẽ** *my new books*

तुम्हारे बड़े कमरे **tumhāre baṛe kamre** *your big rooms*	हमारी सफ़ेद दीवारें **hamārī safed dīvārẽ** *our white walls*
हमारे लाल फूल **hamāre lāl phūl** *our red flowers*	इनकी लम्बी बेटियाँ **inkī lambī beṭiyā̃** *their tall daughters*
उसके काले जूते **uske kāle jūte** *his/her black shoes*	उनकी हरी अलमारियाँ **unkī harī almāriyā̃** *their green cupboards*
उसके लाल दरवाज़े **uske lāl daravāze** *his/her red doors*	उनकी सुन्दर बेटियाँ **unkī sundar beṭiyā̃** *their beautiful daughters*

Work Out 1

5F Work Out 1

Listen to your audio and fill in the blanks with the words that you hear.

1. ____________ लड़कियाँ

   ____________ **laṛkiyā̃**

2. ____________ परदे

   ____________ **pardẽ**

3. ____________ घर

____________ **ghar**

4. ____________ आदमी

____________ **ādmī**

5. ____________ लड़की

____________ **laṛkī**

6. ____________ भाई

____________ **bhāī**

7. ____________ चाय

____________ **cāi**

ANSWER KEY

1. लम्बी **lambī** (*tall girls*); 2. पीले **pīle** (*yellow curtains*); 3. ऊंचे **ũce** (*tall houses*); 4. मोटा **moṭā** (*fat man*); 5. छोटी **choṭī** (*small girl*); 6. बड़ा **baṛā** (*elder brother*); 7. गरम **garam** (*hot tea*)

Bring It All Together

5G Bring It All Together

Now let's listen to some descriptions in a monologue.

यह मेरा नया स्कूल है।
yah merā nayā skul hai.
This is my new school.

इमारत बड़ी है।
īmārat baṛī hai.
The building is large.

बहुत सी नीली खिड़कियाँ भी हैं।
bahut sī nīlī khiṛkiyā̃ bhī haĩ.
There are many blue windows as well.

दरवाज़े बड़े हैं और काले रंग के हैं।
darvāzẽ baṛe haĩ aur kāle rang ke haĩ.
The doors are big and black.

हमारी कक्षा चौड़ी है।
hamārī kakṣā cauṛī hai.
Our classroom is wide.

दीवारें सफ़ेद हैं और छत नीली है।
dīvarẽ safed haĩ aur chat nīlī hai.
The walls are white and the ceiling is blue.

एक ऊंची अलमारी भी है।
ek ūncī almārī bhī hai.
There is a tall cupboard as well.

बाहर एक छोटा बगीचा है।
bāhar ek choṭā bagīcā hai.
Outside, there is a small garden.

उसमे बहुत से सुन्दर फूल हैं।
usme bahut se sundar phūl haĩ.
There are many beautiful flowers in it.

Take It Further 3

5H Take It Further 3

Let's look at the new vocabulary.

कक्षा (*f.*)	**kakṣā**	*classroom*
चौड़ी	**cauṛī**	*wide (f.)*
छत (*f.*)	**chat**	*ceiling*
इमारत (*f.*)	**īmārat**	*building*

Remember that चौड़ी **cauṛī** is an adjective that ends in the sound ई **ī** because it is talking about a feminine subject. If it were to describe a masculine noun, for example **kamrā** *(room)*, it would take the ending आ **ā**. Also remember, it will take the ending ए **e** in case of plural masculine nouns.

चौड़ी दीवार	**cauṛī dīvār**	*wide wall*
चौड़ा कमरा	**cauṛā kamrā**	*wide room*
चौड़े कमरे	**cauṛe kamre**	*wide rooms*
चौड़ी दीवारें	**cauṛī dīvārẽ**	*wide walls*

Work Out 2

Let's practice what you've learned. Fill in the blanks with the missing words.

1. यह ____________ दीवार है।

   yah ____________ dīvār hai.

   This is a white wall.

2. वे ____________ खिड़कियाँ हैं।

   ve ____________ khiṛkiyā̃ haĩ.

   Those are yellow windows.

3. वह ____________ दरवाज़ा है।

   vah ____________ darvāzā hai.

   This is a green door.

4. मेरा भाई ____________ है।

   merā bhāī ____________ hai

   My brother is tall.

5. मेरी बहन ____________ है।

   merī bahan ____________ hai

   My sister is small.

6. चाय ____________ है।

   cai ____________ hai

   The tea is hot.

7. यह दीवार ____________ है।

   yah dīvār ____________ hai

   That is a black wall.

ANSWER KEY

1. सफ़ेद **safed** 2. पीली **pīlī** 3. हरा **harā** 4. लम्बा **lambā** 5. छोटी **choṭī** 6. गरम **garam** 7. काली **kālī**

Drive It Home

Translate the following phrases into Hindi. Remember that the adjective needs to agree with the gender and number of the noun.

1. *tall girls* __________
2. *green windows* __________
3. *black doors* __________
4. *white walls* __________
5. *many brothers* __________
6. *small sisters* __________
7. *beautiful flowers* __________
8. *new school* __________
9. *old home* __________
10. *cold tea* __________
11. *big building* __________
12. *blue color* __________

ANSWER KEY

1. लम्बी लड़कियाँ **lambī laṛkiyā̃** 2. हरी खिड़कियाँ **harī khiṛkiyā̃** 3. काले दरवाज़े **kāle darvāze** 4. सफ़ेद दीवारें **safed dīvārẽ** 5. बहुत से भाई **bahut se bhāī** 6. छोटी बहनें **choṭī bahanẽ** 7. सुन्दर फूल **sundar phūl** 8. नया स्कूल **nayī skūl** 9. पुराना घर **purānā ghar** 10. ठंडी चाय **ṭhandī cāi** 11. बड़ी इमारत **baṛī īmārat** 12. नीला रंग **nīlā rang**

Take It Further 4

Let's review some of the rules of adjective agreement, so when you come across new adjectives, you know how to use them in constructing sentences and describing things around.

1. Adjectives describing masculine nouns usually end in the vowel आ **ā**.
2. When describing feminine nouns, both singular and plural, the adjective will usually end in the vowel ई **ī**.
3. When describing masculine nouns in plural, the adjective will end in the vowel ए **e**.
4. When the plural constitutes a mixed group of masculine and feminine nouns, the adjective will take up the masculine noun ending ए **e**.

Parting Words

You've come to the end of your fifth lesson! By now you should know:

- ☐ Basic adjectives to describe people and objects, both animate and inanimate. (Still unsure? Go back to Vocabulary Builder 1 or Vocabulary Builder 2.)

- ☐ Adjective agreement with singular and plural nouns. (Still unsure? Go back to Grammar Builder 1 or Grammar Builder 2.)
- ☐ Devanagari: Group 5 alphabets: Retroflex consonants: ट ṭa, ठ ṭha, ड ḍa, ढ ḍha. (Still unsure? Go back to Take It Further 1.)

Word Recall

Let's review the most important vocabulary you learned. Match the English in the left column with the Hindi equivalents in the right column.

1. *color* — a. गरम **garam**
2. *big* — b. छोटा **choṭā**
3. *small* — c. नया **nayā**
4. *blue* — d. बड़ा **baṛā**
5. *beautiful* — e. बुरा **burā**
6. *bad* — f. रंग **rang**
7. *hot* — g. नीला **nīlā**
8. *new* — h. सुन्दर **sundar**

ANSWER KEY

1. f; 2. d; 3. b; 4. g; 5. h; 6. e; 7. a; 8. c

Quiz 1

Now let's see how you've done so far. In this section you'll find a short quiz testing what you learned in Lessons 1–5. After you've answered all of the questions, score your quiz and see how you did! If you find that you need to go back and review, please do so before continuing on to Lesson 6.

You'll get a second quiz after Lesson 10, followed by a final review with five dialogues and comprehension questions.

Let's get started!

A. Fill in the blanks with the appropriate forms of the verb होना **hona** (*to be*).

1. *I am* ________________
2. *they/those are* ________________
3. *she is* ________________
4. *we are* ________________
5. *you are* ________________

B. Match the Hindi expressions in the left column with the English equivalents on the right.

1. आपका नाम क्या है? **āpkā nām kyā hai?**	a. *It's all right/no problem.*
2. पिताजी **pitājī**	b. *see you again*

3. कोई बात नहीं। c. *welcome*

koī bāt nahī̃.

4. स्वागत है d. *father*

swagat hai

5. फिर मिलेंगे e. *What's your name?*

phir milẽge

C. Provide the Hindi equivalents in numbers and words, for the following numbers.

1. *four* ______________________
2. *nineteen* ______________________
3. *seven* ______________________
4. *eleven* ______________________
5. *twenty* ______________________

D. Translate the following into Hindi. Pay attention to the gender and number.

1. *my books* ______________________
2. *her sons* ______________________
3. *our sister* ______________________
4. *their brother* ______________________
5. *their curtains* ______________________

ANSWER KEY

A. 1. मैं हूँ maĩ hū̃ 2. वे हैं ve haĩ 3. वह है vah hai 4. हम हैं ham haĩ 5. तुम हो tum ho

B. 1. e; 2. d; 3. a; 4. c; 5. h

C. 1. चार ४ cār 2. उन्नीस १९ unnīs 3. सात ७ sāt 4. ग्यारह ११ gyārah 5. बीस २० bīs

D. 1. मेरी किताबें merī kitābẽ 2. उसके बेटे uske bete 3. हमारी बहन hamārī bahan 4. उनका भाई unkā bhāī 5. उनके परदे unke parde

How Did You Do?

Give yourself a point for every correct answer, then use the following key to determine whether or not you're ready to move on:

0–7 points: It's probably best to go back and study the lessons again to make sure you undersood everything completely. Take your time; it's not a race! Make sure you spend time reviewing the vocabulary and reading through each Grammar Builder section carefully.

8–16 points: You would benefit from a review before moving on. Go back and spend a little more time on the specific points that gave you trouble. Reread the Grammar Builder sections that were difficult and do the Work Outs one more time. Don't forget about the online practice material! Go to **www.livinglanguage.com/languagelab** to reinforce the material from these lessons.

17–20 points: Feel free to move on to Lesson 6! You're doing a great job.

points

Lesson 6: Around Town

पाठ ६: शहर में

pāṭh chah: śahar mẽ

In this lesson, you'll learn expressions and other useful words and phrases that will help you get around a city. You'll learn:

- ☐ Essential vocabulary to help you ask for directions.
- ☐ Questions and phrases to help you find your way and understand directions.
- ☐ How to express location.
- ☐ Devanagari: Group 6 consonants: प **pa**, फ **pha**, ब **ba**, भ **bha**.

Are you ready to begin?

Vocabulary Builder 1

6A Vocabulary Builder 1

उधर	**udhar**	*there*
वहाँ	**vahā̃**	*there*
इधर	**idhar**	*here*
यहाँ	**yahā̃**	*here*

पास	**pās**	*near*
सड़क	**saṛak**	*road (f.)*
गली	**galī**	*street/lane (f.)*
मंदिर	**mandir**	*temple (m.)*
मोड़	**moṛ**	*turn/turning (m.)*
गिरिजाघर/चर्च	**girijāghar/carc**	*church (m.)*
मस्जिद	**masjid**	*mosque (f.)*
पुल	**pul**	*bridge (m.)*
बाज़ार	**bāzār**	*market (m.)*
दुकान	**dukān**	*store/shop (f.)*
डाकघर	**dākghar**	*post office (m.)*
घंटाघर	**ghanṭāghar**	*clock tower (m.)*
चौराहा	**caurāhā**	*intersection (m.)*

Did you notice the two different ways of saying *here* and *there?* Both are interchangeable.

Vocabulary Practice 1

Let's practice the vocabulary that you've learned. Match the Hindi in the first column to the English equivalent in the second.

1. बाज़ार **bāzār**	a. *temple*
2. दुकान **dukān**	b. *road*
3. घंटाघर **ghanṭāghar**	c. *near*
4. मंदिर **mandir**	d. *shop*
5. पास **pās**	e. *market*
6. चौराहा **caurāhā**	f. *clock tower*
7. सड़क **saṛak**	g. *intersection*

ANSWER KEY

1. e; 2. d; 3. f; 4. a; 5. c; 6. g; 7. b

Grammar Builder 1

6B Grammar Builder 1

ASKING QUESTIONS: USING *WHERE, HOW, WHICH*

Do you remember the question words क्या **kyā** (*what*) and कौन **kaun** (*who*) that you learned in Lesson 1? Let's review them quickly.

आपका नाम क्या है?	**āpkā nām kyā hai?**	*What's your name?*
यह आदमी कौन है?	**yah ādmī kaun hai?**	*Who is this man?*

Now let's look at a few other question words that are useful for asking directions and getting around.

किधर?	**kidhar?**	*where?*
मंदिर किधर है?	**mandir kidhar hai?**	*Where is the temple?*
कहाँ?	**kahā̃?**	*where?*
अनवर कहाँ है?	**anwar kahā̃ hai?**	*Where is Anwar?*
कितने?	**kitne?**	*how many?*
कितने मील हैं?	**kitne mīl haĩ?**	*How many miles?*
कौन-सा?	**kaunsā?**	*which?*
यह कौन-सा होटल है?	**yah kaunsā hotal hai?**	*Which hotel is this?*

कितनी दूर?	**kitnī dūr?**	*how far?*
बगीचा कितनी दूर है?	**bagīcā kitnī dūr hai?**	*How far is the garden?*

The two words for *where*, किधर **kidhar** and कहाँ **kahā̃** are interchangeable.

Take It Further 1

Let's look at the Devanagari now. Turn to the *Guide to Reading and Writing Hindi* and cover:

- ☐ Group 6 Consonants: प **pa**, फ **pha**, ब **ba**, भ **bha**

Vocabulary Builder 2

6C Vocabulary Builder 2

...किधर है?	**...kidhar hai?**	*where is...?*
...कितनी दूर है?	**...kitnī dūr hai?**	*how far is the...?*
इधर से	**idhar se**	*from here*
उधर से	**udhar se**	*from there*
मुड़ जाओ	**muṛ jāo**	*take a turn*
दूर	**dūr**	*far (f.)*

दाएँ मुड़ो	**dāyẽ muṛo**	*turn right/take a right turn*
बाएं मुड़ो	**bāyẽ muṛo**	*turn left/take a left turn*
पीछे	**pīche**	*behind*
पेड़	**peṛ**	*tree (m.)*
ऊपर	**ūpar**	*above*
आगे	**āge**	*ahead*
सामने	**sāmne**	*in front*

Vocabulary Practice 2

Translate the following into Hindi.

1. *How far is the temple?*

2. *Where is the shop?*

3. *There is the market. Turn right.*

4. *Turn left.*

5. *This is the mosque.*

6. *That is the church.*

ANSWER KEY

1. मंदिर कितनी दूर है? **mandir kitnī dūr hai?** 2. दुकान किधर है? **dukān kidhar hai?** 3. बाज़ार उधर है। दाएँ मुड़ो। **bāzār udhar hai. dāyẽ muṛo.** 4. बाएं मुड़ो। **bāyẽ muṛo.** 5. यह मस्जिद है। **yah masjid hai.** 6. वह गिरिजाघर है। **vah girijāghar hai.**

Grammar Builder 2

6D Grammar Builder 2

EXPRESSING LOCATION USING SIMPLE POSTPOSITIONS

When you want to express location in English, you use prepositions (*in, on, from, at*). They are called prepositions because they're positioned before (pre-) a noun in English. In Hindi, these words are called postpositions because they come after nouns. There are a few simple postpositions that you'll see in this lesson: में **mẽ** (*in/around*), पर **par** (*on/at*), से **se** (*from*) and तक **tak** (*up till/to*). Let's look at some examples. Notice that they all come after the noun.

दिल्ली में	**dillī mẽ**	*in Delhi*
होटल पर	**hotal par**	*at the hotel*
आगरा से	**āgrā se**	*from Agra*

When you use postpositions in Hindi, the noun is going to change its form, or in grammatical terms, its case. A case is simply the role a noun is playing in a sentence. For example, in *John ate a cookie*, the noun John is playing the role of the subject, so it's in what's called the nominative case. But if John is the direct object, as in *Mary saw John*, then John is in a different case, called accusative case. In some languages, nouns change form depending on their case. This is called a declension, and it involves a different set of endings.

In Hindi, all nouns are in the nominative case when they have the role of a subject in a sentence (this is the form you see in dictionaries). Whenever a noun is followed by a postposition, it's in the oblique case. Many nouns are identical in the nominative and oblique cases. We are going to focus on these nouns in this lesson. We'll come back to nouns that take on different endings in the oblique case later.

Proper nouns—names of people, places and so on—do not change in the oblique. Masculine singular nouns that end in consonants—like होटल **hotal** (*hotel*), पुल **pul** (*bridge*), and सड़क **saṛak** (*road*) also do not change in the oblique. Let's look at some examples of sentences with postpositions.

में **mẽ** *in/around*	वह दिल्ली में है।	**vah dillī mẽ hai.**	*He is in Delhi.*
	होटल में कमरे हैं।	**hotal mẽ kamre haĩ.**	*There are rooms in the hotel.*
	बर्तन में चाय है।	**bartan mẽ cāi hai.**	*There is tea in the pot.*

पर par *on/at*	नदी पर एक पुल है।	**nadī par ek pul hai.**	*There is a bridge on (over) the river.*
	मोड़ पर एक बगीचा है।	**moṛ par ek bagīcā hai.**	*There is a garden at the turn.*
	किताब पर सेब है।	**kitāb par seb hai.**	*There is an apple on the book.*
से se *from*	बगीचा सड़क से दायें है।	**bagīcā saṛak se dāyẽ hai.**	*The garden is to the right of the road.*
	डाकघर होटल से सीधे है।	**dākghar hotal se sīdhe hai.**	*The post office is straight down the street from the hotel.*
	राम दिल्ली से है।	**rām dillī se hai.**	*Ram is from Delhi.*
तक tak *up till/to*	होटल तक	**hotal tak**	*up to the hotel*
	डाकघर से होटल तक	**dākghar se hotal tak**	*from the post office to the hotel*
	बगीचा उधर तक है।	**bagīcā udhar tak hai.**	*The garden stretches (is) up to there (that place).*

Take It Further 2

6E Take It Further 2

COMPOUND POSTPOSITIONS

You just learned about simple postpositions in Grammar Builder 2. In Hindi, there are also compound postpositions, meaning that they consist of two or more words. The first part of the compound can be के **ke** which is a different form of का **kā**, which you already know is used for possession, like in **āpkā** *yours*.

When talking about inanimate possession, के **ke** (*of/indicates belonging*) can be combined with adverbs to form a compound postpositions such as के पीछे **ke pīche** (*behind [lit.: behind of]*), के पास **ke pās** (*near [lit.: near of]*), के आगे **ke āge** (*ahead/front of*).

Postpositions and the Hindi word order

The Hindi word order, as you already learned, is Subject + Object + Verb. However, this order is flexible, and can change when used with postpositions, depending upon which part of the sentence the speaker wants to emphasize.

Just like in the other examples in this lesson, we will use nouns that retain their nominative form.

The following sentence is in Subject + Object + Verb order.

राम किताब पढ़ता है।	**rām kitāb paṛhtā hai.**	*Ram reads a book.*

However, depending on the context, the word order can change:

किताब राम पढ़ता है।	**kitāb rām paṛhtā hai.**	*Ram is the one that reads the book (and not somebody else.)*

In Hindi, this switch happens when the speaker wants to emphasize something or focus on something and moves it to the sentence-initial position. This change is dependent on context, and used mostly at the speaker's discretion.

Let's look at some more compound postpositions usage. The following sentences focus on landmarks, and illustrate the flexibility of the Hindi word order.

Keep in mind that in Hindi, postpositions, or compound postpositions, will be followed by the word that they modify.

पुल के पास	**pul ke pās**	*near the bridge*
पुल के पास होटल है।	**pul ke pās hotal hai.**	*There is a hotel near the bridge.*
स्कूल के पीछे	**skūl ke pīche**	*behind the school*
स्कूल के पीछे मैदान है।	**skūl ke pīche maidān hai.**	*The ground/field is behind the school.*
स्कूल के आगे	**skūl ke āge**	*in front of the school*
स्कूल के आगे मैदान है।	**skūl ke āge maidān hai.**	*The ground/field is in front of the school.*

Work Out 1

6F Work Out 1

Listen to your audio and fill in the blanks with the words that you hear.

1. होटल ________________ है?

   hotal ________________ hai?

2. बगीचा ________________ है।

   bagīcā ________________ hai.

3. यह बड़ी ________________ है।

   yah baṛī ________________ hai.

4. ________________ मंदिर के पास है।

   ________________ mandir ke pās hai.

5. गिरिजाघर ________________ है।

   girijāghar ________________ hai.

6. फूलों का ________________ सुन्दर है।

   phūlõ kā ________________ sundar hai.

7. संग्रहालय पांच मिनट ________________ है।

   sangrahālay pā̃c minit ________________ hai.

ANSWER KEY

1. किधर **kidhar** (*Where is the hotel?*) 2. पास **pās** (*The garden is near.*) 3. सड़क **saṛak** (*This is a main road.* 4. घंटाघर **ghantāghar** (*The clock tower is near the temple.*) 5. दाएँ **dāyẽ** (*The church is to the right.*) 6. बगीचा **bagīcā** (*The flower garden is beautiful.*) 7. दूर **dūr** (*The museum is 5 minutes away.*)

Bring It All Together

6G Bring It All Together

Mahesh has just arrived in a new city for the first time. He would like to do some sight-seeing. Let's listen in as he talks to the Tourism Department representative.

Representative: हमारे शहर में आपका स्वागत है।
hamāre śahar mẽ āpkā svāgat hai.
Welcome to our city.

Mahesh: धन्यवाद। क्या यहाँ देखने के लिए कोई अच्छी जगह है?
dhanyavād. kyā yahā̃ dekhne ke liye koī acchī jagah hai?
Thank you. Is there a good place for sightseeing here?

Representative: हाँ। संग्रहालय और फूलों का बगीचा है।
hā̃. sangrahālay aur phūlõ kā bagīcā hai.
Yes. There is the museum and the flower garden.

Mahesh: बहुत अच्छे। संग्रहालय जाने का रास्ता क्या है?
bahut acche. sangrahālay jāne ka rāstā kyā hai?
Very good. Which way to the museum? (lit.: What is the way to the museum?)

Representative: सामने एक बड़ी सड़क है। सौ मीटर आगे एक चौराहा है। वहां आप बाएं मुड़िए। संग्रहालय पांच मिनट दूर है।
sāmne ek baṛī saṛak hai. sau mītar āge ek caurāhā hai. vahā̃ āp bāyẽ muṛiye. sangrahālay pā̃c minit dūr hai.
There's a main road in front (here). There is an intersection 100 meters ahead. Turn left there. The museum is five minutes away.

Mahesh: समझा। बगीचा किधर है?
samjhā. bagīcā kidhar hai?
I understand. Where is the garden?

Representative: बगीचा बड़े बाज़ार के पास है। बड़े बाज़ार में एक घंटाघर है। घंटाघर से दायें मुड़िए। उधर एक बड़ा पुल है। पुल से बाएं बगीचा है।
bagīcā baṛe bāzār ke pās hai. baṛe bāzār mẽ ek ghantāghar hai. ghantāghar se dāyẽ muṛiye. udhar ek baṛa pul hai. pul se bāyẽ bagīcā hai.
The garden is near the big market. There is a clock tower in the big market. Turn right at the clock tower. There is a big bridge there. The garden is to the left of the bridge.

Mahesh: जी धन्यवाद।
jī dhanyavād.
Ok. Thank you.

Take It Further 3

6H Take It Further 3

In the above dialogue, notice that the adjective बड़ा **baṛā** (*big*) is in the oblique form. You'll learn more about the oblique case in Lesson 9. For now, just note that बड़ा **baṛā** (*big*) is in the oblique form because the noun that it is describing, बाज़ार **bāzār** (*market*), is followed by a compound postposition के पास **ke pās** (*near*) in the first sentence, and the postposition में **mẽ** (*in*) in the second sentence.

बगीचा बड़े बाज़ार के पास है।	**bagīcā baṛe bāzār ke pās hai.**	*The garden is near the big market.*
बड़े बाज़ार में एक घंटाघर है।	**baṛe bāzār mẽ ek ghantāghar hai.**	*There is a clock tower in the big market.*

Work Out 2

Let's practice what you've learned. Fill in the blanks with the missing words.

1. डाकघर ____________ है?

   dākghar ____________ hai?

   Where is the post office?

2. स्कूल ____________ दूर है?

   skūl ____________ dūr hai?

   How far is the school?

3. चौराहा होटल ____________ है।

   caurāhā hotal ____________ hai.

   The intersection is near the hotel.

4. अजय का घर ____________ के पीछे है।

   ajay kā ghar ____________ ke pīche hai.

   Ajay's house is behind the river.

5. बाज़ार से ________________ मुड़ो।

bāzār se ________________ muṛo.

Turn left at the market.

6. ________________ सड़क से दाएँ है।

________________ **saṛak se dāyẽ hai.**

The clock tower is to the right of the road.

7. पुल नदी के ________________ है।

pul nadī ke ________________ hai.

The bridge is over the river.

ANSWER KEY

1. किधर **kidhar** 2. कितनी **kitnī** 3. के पास **ke pās** 4. नदी **nadī** 5. बाएं **bāyẽ** 6. घंटाघर **ghantāghar** 7. ऊपर **ūpar**

Drive It Home

Let's practice asking for directions using किधर **kidhar**, कहाँ **kahā̃**, कितना **kitnā**, कितनी **kitnī**, कौन-सा **kaunsā**. Translate using the appropriate question word. Remember, किधर **kidhar** and कहाँ **kahā̃** are interchangeable, so don't worry just yet, if you don't find your answer matching with that in the key.

1. *Where is the school?*

____

2. *Where is Hotel Minerva?*

____

3. *How far is the bridge?*

4. *Which road is this?*

5. *How many houses are there (in this place)?*

6. *Which house is Seema's (belongs to Seema)?*

ANSWER KEY

1. स्कूल किधर है? **skūl kidhar hai?** 2. होटल मिनर्वा कहाँ है? **hotal minarvā kahā̃ hai?** 3. पुल कितनी दूर है? **pul kitnī dūr hai?** 4. यह कौन-सी सड़क है? **yah kaunsī saṛak hai?** 5. यहाँ कितने घर है? **yahā̃ kitne ghar hai?** 6. सीमा का घर कौनसा है? **sīma kā ghar kaunsā hai?**

Culture Note

Indian cities and towns are often made up of asymmetric neighborhoods. This is because most of them are old cities that have evolved with time. Many modern cities, or parts of them, still reflect their original town planning patterns. As a result, houses are not always set in an orderly fashion, and finding an address is often dependent on landmarks. The smaller the town, the smaller the landmarks; for example, even a spreading banyan tree can become a landmark in a locality of around 50 houses.

Newer parts of the city/town could be more orderly with addresses comprising blocks and apartment numbers. However, landmarks like bridges, crossroads, post offices, schools, etc., play an important role in locating any address.

Parting Words

You've come to the end of your sixth lesson! By now you should know:

- ☐ Essential vocabulary to help you ask for directions. (Still unsure? Go back to Vocabulary Builder 1 or Vocabulary Builder 2.)
- ☐ Questions and phrases to help you find your way and understand directions. (Still unsure? Go back to Grammar Builder 1.)
- ☐ How to express location. (Still unsure? Go back to Grammar Builder 2.)
- ☐ Devanagari: Group 6 consonants: प **pa**, फ **pha**, ब **ba**, भ **bha**. (Still unsure? Go back to Take It Further 1.)

Word Recall

Let's review the most important vocabulary you learned in Lesson 6. Match the Hindi words in the left column with their English equivalents in the right column.

1. पास **pās**	a. *how far*
2. ऊपर **ūpar**	b. *clock tower*
3. कितनी दूर **kitnī dūr**	c. *road*
4. इसके पीछे **iske pīche**	d. *near*
5. सड़क **saṛak**	e. *turn left*
6. घंटाघर **ghantāghar**	f. *behind this*
7. बाएँ मुड़ो **bāyẽ muṛo**	g. *above*

ANSWER KEY

1. d; 2. g; 3. a; 4. f; 5. c; 6. b; 7. e

Lesson 7: At the Restaurant

पाठ ७: रेस्तरां में

pāṭh sāt: restarā̃ mẽ

In this lesson, you'll learn basic expressions and useful words you can use at a restaurant. You'll learn:

- ☐ Essential vocabulary to get by in a restaurant.
- ☐ How to express quantities.
- ☐ How to make polite requests.
- ☐ How to express your likes and dislikes.
- ☐ Devanagari: Nasals ङ ṅa, ञ ña, ण ṇa, न na, म m.

Vocabulary Builder 1

7A Vocabulary Builder 1

जगह	**jagah**	*place (f.)*
पानी	**pānī**	*water (m.)*
थाली	**thālī**	*plate (f..)*
खाना	**khānā**	*food (m.)*

चाहिए	**cāhiye**	*want*
मेनू	**menyu**	*menu (m.)*
चम्मच	**cammac**	*spoon (m.)*
पसंद करना	**pasand karnā**	*like*
शाकाहारी	**śākāhārī**	*vegetarian*
मांसाहारी	**mā̃sāhārī**	*non-vegetarian*
तीखा	**tīkhā**	*spicy (hot)*
जल्दी	**jaldī**	*quickly*

Vocabulary Practice 1

Let's practice the vocabulary that you've learned. Match the French in the first column to the English equivalent in the second.

1. चम्मच
cammac
2. के साथ
ke sāth
3. पानी
pānī

a. *quickly*
b. *plate*
c. *spoon*

4. थाली
   thālī

5. जल्दी
   jaldī

6. जगह
   jagah

7. तीखा
   tīkhā

8. ज़्यादा
   zyādā

d. *spicy*

e. *with*

f. *water*

g. *more*

h. *place*

ANSWER KEY

1. c.; 2. e; 3. f; 4. b; 5. a; 6. h; 7. d; 8. g

Grammar Builder 1

7B Grammar Builder 1

TALKING ABOUT QUANTITIES

Let's look at how to talk about quantities in Hindi.

एक	**ek**	*one*
कुछ	**kuch**	*few*
कम	**kam**	*less*

थोड़ा	**thoṛā**	*little/some*
ज़्यादा	**zyādā**	*more*
और	**aur**	*and/more*
बस	**bas**	*enough*

Let's see how these adjectives are used in sentences.

यह ज़्यादा तीखा है।	**yah zyādā tīkhā hai.**	*This is more spicy.*
और तीखा चाहिए।	**aur tīkhā cāhiye.**	*. . . would like it more spicy.*
कम तेल चाहिए।	**kam tel cāhiye.**	*. . . want less oil.*
थोड़ा पानी चाहिए।	**thoṛā pānī cāhiye.**	*. . . want some water.*
यह बस है।	**yah bas hai.**	*This is enough.*
मुझको एक और रोटी चाहिए।	**mujhko ek aur roṭī cāhīye.**	*I would like one more roti.*

Take It Further 1

Turn to the *Guide to Reading and Writing Hindi* and cover:

☐ Group 7 consonants: nasals **ङ ṅa**, **ञ ña**, **ण ṇa**, **न na**, **म ma**

Vocabulary Builder 2

7C Vocabulary Builder 2

यह स्वादिष्ट है।	**yah swādiṣṭ hai.**	*This is delicious.*
खाने के लिए क्या है?	**khāne ke liye kyā hai?**	*What is there on the menu?*
माहौल	**māhaul**	*ambience (m.)*
चावल	**cāval**	*rice (m.)*
रोटी	**roṭī**	*bread/roti (f.)*
सब्ज़ी	**sabzī**	*vegetable (f.)/ a dish of vegetables*
ज़्यादा	**zyādā**	*more*
यह लो	**yah lo**	*...have this...*
कुछ मीठा	**kuch mīṭhā**	*some dessert (lit.: something sweet)*
नाश्ता	**nāśtā**	*snack (m.)*
गोश्त	**gosht**	*meat (m.)*
दाल	**dāl**	*lentils (f.)*
बस, धन्यवाद	**bas, dhanyavād**	*enough, thanks*

Take It Further 2

7D Take It Further 2

Prepared food items or dishes, especially vegetables and meat are referred to by their names, and at times, by the way they have been cooked. Thus, lentils are called दाल **dāl**, whether cooked into a dish, or uncooked. सब्ज़ी **sabzī** (*vegetable*) is often preceded by the name of the vegetable itself, like आलू की सब्ज़ी **ālu kī sabzī** (*dish made of potatoes*), गोश्त **gosht** (*meat*) may be further qualified मुर्गी का गोश्त **murgī kā gosht** (lit.: *meat of chicken*) or सूअर का गोश्त **sūar kā gosht** (*pork*; lit.: *meat of pig*).

However, in the case of meat, English words, like *chicken*, *mutton*, *pork*, etc., are more commonly used as loanwords now.

The table below lists some terms used commonly.

गोभी मटर की सब्ज़ी **gobhī maṭar kī sabzī** *(a dish of cooked) cauliflower and peas*	पालक **pālak** *spinach/a dish of cooked spinach*
दम के आलू **dam ke ālū** *potatoes cooked 'dum' style*	भुना गोश्त **bhunā gosht** *roast meat*
मूंग की दाल **mū̃g kī dāl** *a type of lentil called 'Moong'/ a dish of cooked Moong*	मक्के की रोटी **makke kī roṭī** *roti made of corn ground into flour*

✎ Vocabulary Practice 2

Translate the following into Hindi.

1. *What would you like to eat?*

___

2. *I would like a dish of rice.*

___

3. *Nothing, thanks.*

___

4. *Here is a plate.*

___

5. *We want a bigger table.*

___

6. *This dish of vegetables is delicious.*

___

7. *Try this dessert.*

___

ANSWER KEY

1. आप क्या खाओगे? **āp kyā khāoge?** 2. मुझे एक प्लेट चावल चाहिए। **mujhe ek plet cāval cāhiye** 3. बस कुछ नहीं। **bas kuch nahĩ** 4. यह प्लेट है। **yah plet hai** 5. हमें बड़ा टेबल चाहिए। **hamẽ baṛā tebal cāhiye** 6. यह सब्ज़ी स्वादिष्ट है। **yah sabzī swādiṣṭ hai.** 7. यह मीठा लो। **yah mīṭhā lo.**

Grammar Builder 2

7E Grammar Builder 2

AN INTRODUCTION TO THE OBLIQUE CASE WHEN EXPRESSING *WANT* AND *LIKE*

Expressing *To Me*

In Hindi, when you want to express that you *want* or *like* something—for example, *I like candy*—you will say *To me, candy is pleasing.* This is how Hindi expresses the concept of liking and wanting. Notice that English uses the preposition *to*. Hindi is no different and it uses the postposition को **ko** (*for/to*). As you learned in Lesson 6, when a word is followed by a postposition, the word is in the oblique case. When a pronoun is followed by postposition को **ko**, the pronoun will be in oblique case, as seen in the examples below.

NOMINATIVE FORM OF POSSESSIVE	OBLIQUE FORM OF POSSESSIVE + को KO
मेरा **merā** *mine*	मेरे को **mere ko** *to me*
हमारा **hamārā** *ours*	हमारे को **hamāre ko** *to us*
तुम्हारा **tumhārā** *yours*	तुम्हारे को **tumhāre ko** *to you*

In the case of हमारा **hamārā**, तुम्हारा **tumhārā**, and other third-person pronouns like इनका **inkā** (*theirs/of these*) or उनका **unkā** (*theirs/of those*), a shorter form is used. Turn to Lessons 2 and 3 for a detailed list of singular and plural possessives.

हमको **hamko** *to us*	तुमको **tumko** *to you*	इनको **inko** *to these*	उनको **unko** *to those*

Let's look at the subject pronouns with को **ko** in more detail.

मुझको	**mujhko**	*to me*
तुमको	**tumko**	*to you*
आपको	**āpko**	*to you*
इसको	**isko**	*to her/him/this one*
उसको	**usko**	*to her/him/that one*
हमको	**hamko**	*to us*
उनको	**unko**	*to them/those*
इनको	**inko**	*to them/these*

When expressing *to want/to need* or a desire to have something, you can use this pattern:

subject pronoun + को ko (*for/to*) + the verb चाहना cāhanā (*to want*)

The verb चाहना cāhanā is the infinitive. The form that you use when you say *I want*, is चाहिए cāhiye. Let's look at some examples:

मुझको...चाहिए।	**mujhko...cāhiye.**	*I want.../I would like to have...*
आपको क्या चाहिए?	**āpko kyā cāhiye?**	*What do you want?*
उसको क्या चाहिए?	**usko kyā cāhiye?**	*What does she want?*
उनको क्या चाहिए?	**unko kyā cāhiye?**	*What do they want?*
उसको...चाहिए	**usko...cāhiye.**	*She wants...*

Expressing *Like/Love*

The Hindi word for *like* is पसंद pasand. To form sentences with पसंद pasand use this pattern:

subject pronoun + को ko (*for/to*) + पसंद pasand +form of the verb होना honā (*to be*).

Take a look at these examples:

मुझको सब्ज़ियाँ पसंद है।	**mujhko sabziyā̃ pasand hai.**	*I like vegetables.*
मुझको पानी पीना पसंद है।	**mujhko pānī pīnā pasand hai.**	*I like to drink water.*

मुझको यह रेस्तरां पसंद है।	**mujhko yah restarā̃ pasand hai.**	*I like this restaurant.*
मुझको राधा पसंद है।	**mujhko rādhā pasand hai.**	*I like Radha.*

Work Out 1

7F Work Out 1

Listen to your audio and fill in the blanks with the words that you hear.

1. मुझको एक ________________ चाहिए।

   mujhko ek ________________ cāhiye.

2. कृपया ________________ दीजिए।

   kṛipayā ________________ dījiye.

3. यह ________________ है।

   yah ________________ hai.

4. उसको सब्ज़ियाँ ________________ है।

   usko sabziyā̃ ________________ hai.

5. उनको थोड़ा ________________ चाहिए।

   unko thoṛā ________________ cāhiye.

6. उसको ________________ चाहिए।

   usko ________________ cāhiye.

7. हम ________________ हैं।

ham ________________ **haĩ.**

ANSWER KEY

1. प्लेट **plet** (*I need a plate.*) 2. नमक **namak** (*Please pass me the salt.*) 3. कुर्सी **kursī** (*This is a chair.*) 4. पसंद **pasand** (*She likes vegetables.*) 5. चावल **cāval** (*They want some rice.*) 6. चम्मच **cammac** (*He wants a spoon.*) 7. शाकाहारी **śākāhārī** (*We are vegetarian.*)

Bring It All Together

7G Bring It All Together

Now let's listen to a short monologue about a restaurant, describing food items, and making requests:

यह एक रेस्तरां है।
yah ek restarā̃ hai.
This is a restaurant.

वह एक कुर्सी है।
vah ek kursī hai.
That is a chair.

यहाँ खाने को क्या मिलेगा?
yahā̃ khāne ko kyā milegā?
What do you get here to eat?

सब्ज़ियाँ हैं। दाल है। अलग अलग रोटियाँ हैं। सलाद है। दही है।
sabziyā̃ haĩ. dāl hai. alag alag rotiyā̃ haĩ. salād hai. dahi hai.
There are vegetables. There is dal. There are different kinds of breads. There is salad. There is curd.

मुझे थोड़ा पानी चाहिए।
mujhe thoṛa pānī cāhiye.
I'd like some water.

मुझे एक सब्ज़ी और कुछ रोटियाँ चाहिए। बस।
mujhe ek sabzī aur kuch rotiyā̃ cāhiye. bas.
I want one vegetable dish and some bread. That's all.

उसको चावल और गोश्त पसंद है।
usko cāval aur gosht pasand hai.
She likes rice and meat.

यह आपका खाना है।
yah āpka khānā hai.
This is your food.

यह सब्ज़ी लो।
yah sabzī lo.
Have this vegetable dish.

सब्ज़ी तीखी है। मुझे थोड़ा पानी दो।
sabzī tīkhī hai. mujhe thoṛa pānī do.
The vegetable dish is spicy (hot). Give me some water.

खाना बहुत स्वादिष्ट है।
khānā bahut swādiṣṭ hai.
The food is delicious.

Take It Further 3

7H Take It Further 3

Notice two new expressions: लो **lo** (*take/have*) and दो **do** (*give*). These are the imperative forms of the verbs लेना **lenā** (*to take*) and देना **denā** (*to give*). When asking for something specifically, लो **lo** and दो **do** are used at the end of a sentence; this form replaces the verb होना **honā** (*to be*). Let's look at a few imperative constructions with these verbs. The form लो **lo** is also used to mean *have* (lit.: *Please take/try.*)

मुझको चावल दो।	**mujhko cāval do.**	*Give me rice.*
एक रोटी दो।	**ek roṭī do.**	*Give one roti.*
थोड़ा पानी लो।	**thoṛā pānī lo.**	*Take some water.*
कुछ मीठा लो।	**kuch mīṭhā lo.**	*Take/Have some dessert.*

Work Out 2

Let's practice what you've learned. Fill in the blanks with the missing words. Note the adjective agreement with the gender and quantity of the noun.

1. मुझको थोड़े ____________ चाहिए।

   mujhko thoṛe ____________ cāhiye.

   I'd like some rice.

2. उसको ________________ पानी चाहिए।

usko ________________ pānī cāhiye.

She wants some water.

3. हमको दो ________________ चाहिए।

hamko do ________________ cāhiye.

We want two places (to sit).

4. उनको दो ________________ और थोड़ा चावल चाहिए।

unko do ________________ aur thoṛa cāval cāhiye.

They want two vegetables and some rice.

5. उसको थोड़ा ________________ चाहिए।

usko thoṛa ________________ cāhiye.

She wants some salt.

6. हमको ________________ चाहिए।

hamko ________________ hai.

We want food.

7. वे ________________ हैं।

ve ________________ haĩ.

They are non-vegetarian.

ANSWER KEY

1. चावल **cāval** 2. थोड़ा **thoṛa** 3. जगह **jagah** 4. सब्ज़ियाँ **sabziyā̃** 5. नमक **namak** 6. खाना **khānā** 7. मांसाहारी **mā̃sāhārī**

Drive It Home

Let's practice the different forms of the verb चाहना **cāhanā**. Translate the following expressions, using the appropriate form of चाहना:

1. *What do you want?*

2. *I want.*

3. *She wants.*

4. *They want.*

5. *He wants.*

6. *We want.*

7. *You want.*

ANSWER KEY

1. आपको क्या चाहिए? **āpko kyā cāhiye?** 2. मुझे चाहिए **mujhe cāhiye** 3. उसको चाहिए **usko cāhiye** 4. उनको चाहिए **unko cāhiye** 5. उसको चाहिए **usko cāhiye** 6. हमको चाहिए **hamko cāhiye** 7. तुमको चाहिए **tumko cāhiye**

Parting Words

You've come to the end of the lesson. By now you should know how to:

- ☐ Essential vocabulary to get by in a restaurant. (Still unsure? Go back to Vocabulary Builder 1 or Vocabulary Builder 2.)
- ☐ How to express quantities. (Still unsure? Go back to Grammar Builder 1.)
- ☐ How to make polite requests. (Still unsure? Go back to Grammar Builder 2.)
- ☐ How to express your likes and dislikes. (Still unsure? Go back to Grammar Builder 2.)
- ☐ Devanagari: Nasals ङ ṅa, ञ ña, ण ṇa, न na, म ma. (Still unsure? Go back to Take It Further 1.)

Word Recall

Let's review the most important vocabulary you learned in Lesson 1. Match the Hindi

1. चम्मच
   cammac
2. स्वादिष्ट
   swādiṣṭ
3. तीखा
   tīkhā
4. पीने का पानी
   pīne kā pānī
5. खाना
   khānā
6. प्लेट
   plet
7. जगह
   jagah

a. *delicious*

b. *food*

c. *plate*

d. *spoon*

e. *place*

f. *spicy*

g. *drinking water*

ANSWER KEY

1. d; 2. a; 3. f; 4. g; 5. b; 6. c; 7. e

Lesson 8: At the Marketplace

पाठ ८: बाज़ार में

pāṭh āṭh: bāzār mẽ

This lesson is all about shopping. You'll learn:

- ☐ Vocabulary related to shopping/buying.
- ☐ How to express *want*, *take*, *give*, etc. when out shopping.
- ☐ The present imperfective.
- ☐ Devanagari: Group 7 & 8 consonants: श śa, ष ṣa, स sa, र ra, ड़ ṛa, ढ़ ṛha.

Are you ready to begin?

Vocabulary Builder 1

8A Vocabulary Builder 1

दुकान	**dukān**	*store (f.)*
कपड़ा	**kapṛā**	*cloth/fabric (m.)*
कपड़े	**kapṛe**	*clothes (m.)*
कितने हुए	**kitne hue?**	*how much?*

कीमत	kīmat	*price (f.)*
और दिखाइए	aur dikhāiye	*show more*
महंगा	mahãngā	*expensive*
सस्ता	sastā	*cheap*
बच्चों के कपड़े	baccõ ke kapṛe	*children's clothes*
जूते	jūte	*shoes (m.)*
दूसरा	dūsrā	*another one*
दिखाओ	dikhāo	*please show*
कुछ	kuch	*something*

Vocabulary Practice 1

Let's practice the vocabulary that you've learned. Match the Hindi in the first column to the English equivalent in the second.

1. दुकान
   dukān
2. महंगा
   mahãngā
3. बच्चों के कपड़े
   baccõ ke kapṛe

a. *shoes*

b. *store*

c. *how much?*

4. और दिखाइए
   aur dikhāiye

d. *children's clothes*

5. जूते
   jūte

e. *cheap*

6. सस्ता
   sastā

f. *show another one*

7. कितने हुए
   kitne hue?

g. *expensive*

ANSWER KEY

1. b; 2. g; 3. d; 4. f; 5. a; 6. e; 7. c

Grammar Builder 1

8B Grammar Builder 1

MAKING COMPARISONS

When you want to indicate more of something, like the English *-er* (*bigger*, *smaller*, etc.) Hindi uses the word और **aur** (*and*) before an adjective. Let's look at a few Hindi expressions using और **aur**.

सस्ता **sastā** *cheap*	और सस्ता **aur sastā** *cheaper*

महंगा **mahãngā** *expensive*	और महंगा **aur mahãngā** *more expensive*
बड़ा **baṛā** *large*	और बड़ा **aur baṛā** *larger*
छोटा **choṭā** *small*	और छोटा **aur choṭā** *smaller*
अच्छा **acchā** *good*	और अच्छा **aur acchā** *better*

In the last lesson you learned how to use the verb चाहना **cāhanā** (*to want*). Let's look at some examples using चाहना **cāhanā**. Notice the plural form of the adjectives as you go along.

मुझको महंगे कपड़े चाहिए।	**mujhko mahãnge kapṛe cāhiye.**	*I want expensive clothes.*
उसको और महंगे कपड़े चाहिए।	**usko aur mahãnge kapṛe cāhiye.**	*He wants more expensive clothes.*
मुझको छोटा कपड़ा चाहिए।	**mujhko choṭā kapṛā cāhiye.**	*I want a (piece of) small cloth.*

उसको और छोटा कपड़ा चाहिए।	**usko aur choṭā kapṛā cāhiye.**	*She wants a smaller (piece of) cloth.*
उसको सस्ता जूता चाहिए।	**usko sastā jūtā cāhiye.**	*He wants a cheap shoe.*
उनको सस्ते कपड़े चाहिए।	**unko saste kapṛe cāhiye.**	*They want cheap clothes.*

Take It Further 1

Let's take a closer look at Devanagari now. Turn to the *Guide to Reading and Writing Hindi* and cover:

☐ Group 7 & 8 alphabets: श **śa**, ष **ṣa**, स **sa**, र **ra**, ड़ **ṛa**, ढ़ **ṛha**

Vocabulary Builder 2

8C Vocabulary Builder 2

खरीदना	**kharīdnā**	*to buy*
कुछ सामान	**kuch sāmān**	*some stuff/things (m)*
कुछ	**kuch**	*something*
देखो	**dekho**	*look (imperative)*
अच्छा है	**acchā hai**	*nice/looks nice*
कमीज़	**kamīz**	*shirt (f)*

कुर्ता	**kurtā**	*tunic (f)*
दुपट्टा	**dupaṭṭā**	*stole (m)*
पतलून	**patlūn**	*trousers (f)*

Take It Further 2

8D Take It Further 2

The word कुछ **kuch** (*something*) has many different uses depending on the context. For now, let's look at two examples:

कुछ नया दिखाओ।	**kuch nayā dikhāo.**	*Show something new.*
कुछ सस्ता दिखाओ।	**kuch sastā dikhāo.**	*Show something cheap.*

You saw two imperative forms in Lesson 7: लो **lo** (*take*) and दो **do** (*give*). Similarly, खरीदो **kharīdo** (*buy*) and दिखाओ **dikhāo** (*show*) are imperative forms of the verbs खरीदना **kharīdnā** (*to buy*) and दिखाना **dikhānā** (*to show*). Like the previous imperatives, these forms are also placed at the end of a sentence and they replace the verb होना **honā** (*to be*).

एक नीला कुर्ता खरीदो।	**ek nīlā kurtā kharīdo.**	*Buy a blue tunic.*
नई कमीज़ खरीदो।	**nayī kamīz kharīdo.**	*Buy a new shirt.*
मुझको लाल जूते दिखाओ।	**mujhko lāl jūte dikhāo.**	*Show me red shoes.*

उनको दुकान दिखाओ।	**unko dukān dikhāo.**	*Show them the store.*

Vocabulary Practice 2

Match the English expressions on the left with the Hindi equivalents on the right.

1. *cheaper*	a. दुकान **dukān**
2. *price*	b. अच्छा है **acchā hai**
3. *shoes*	c. कुर्ता **kurtā**
4. *store*	d. जूते **jūte**
5. *shirt*	e. और सस्ता **aur sastā**
6. *looks nice*	f. कमीज़ **kamīz**
7. *tunic*	g. कीमत **kīmat**

ANSWER KEY

1. e; 2 g; 3. d; 4. a; 5. f; 6. b; 7. c

Grammar Builder 2

8E Grammar Builder 2

THE PRESENT IMPERFECTIVE

You have learned a little bit about the present imperfective in earlier lessons. It's used to express a habitual or general action, like the English simple present *I go* or *she speaks*.

You already know that you need two elements: a form of the main verb known as the imperfective participle and the appropriate form of the verb होना **honā** (*to be*) which you are very familiar with.

Now let's take a closer look at forming the imperfective participle, which is derived from the infinitive. In Hindi, the infinitive form of a verb is one word, and it ends with –ना **–nā**:

लेना	**lenā**	*to take*
देना	**denā**	*to give*

The imperfective participle is formed by removing the –ना **–nā** ending from the infinitive, which leaves you with a verb stem (ले **le**, दे **de**). Then, onto this stem you add endings that are very similar to the endings you learned for adjectives. The form of the participle you use depends on the gender and number of the subject. Take a look at the table below which includes all four endings of the verbs लेना **lenā** (*to take*) and देना **denā** (*to give*).

INFINITIVE	M. SINGULAR	F. SINGULAR	M. PLURAL	F. PLURAL
लेना **lenā** *to take*	लेता **letā**	लेती **letī**	लेते **lete**	लेती **letī**
देना **denā** *to give*	देता **detā**	देती **detī**	देते **dete**	देती **detī**

Now let's see what this looks like with subject pronouns. Remember that the pronouns for *I*, *you*, *we* and so forth can be masculine or feminine depending on who you're speaking to. And in the case of a group that includes people of both sexes, the masculine plural form is used.

लेना LENĀ *(TO TAKE)*

MASCULINE	FEMININE
मैं लेता हूँ। **maĩ letā hū̃.** *I take.*	मैं लेती हूँ। **maĩ letī hū̃.** *I take.*
तुम लेते हो। **tum lete ho.** *You take.*	तुम लेती हो। **tum letī ho.** *You take.*

आप लेते हो। **āp lete ho.** *You take.*	आप लेती हो। **āp letī ho.** *You take.*
हम लेते हैं। **ham lete haĩ.** *We take.*	हम लेती हैं। **ham letī haĩ.** *We take.*
वह लेता है। **vah letā hai.** *He takes.*	वह लेती है। **vah letī hai.** *She takes.*
वे लेते हैं। **ve lete haĩ.** *They take.*	वे लेती हैं। **ve letī haĩ.** *They take.*
यह लेता है। **yah letā hai.** *He (this one) takes.*	यह लेती है। **yah letī hai.** *She (this one) takes.*
ये लेते हैं। **ye lete haĩ.** *They (these) take.*	ये लेती हैं। **ye letī haĩ.** *They (these) take.*

देना DENĀ (*TO GIVE*)

MASCULINE	FEMININE
मैं देता हूँ। **maĩ detā hū̃.** *I give.*	मैं देती हूँ। **maĩ detī hū̃.** *I give.*
तुम देते हो। **tum dete ho.** *You give.*	तुम देती हो। **tum detī ho.** *You give.*
आप देते हो। **āp dete ho.** *You give.*	आप देती हो। **āp detī ho.** *You give.*
हम देते हैं। **ham dete haĩ.** *We give.*	हम देती हैं। **ham detī haĩ.** *We give.*
वह देता है। **vah detā hai.** *He gives.*	वह देती है। **vah detī hai.** *She gives.*
वे देते हैं। **ve dete haĩ.** *They give.*	वे देती हैं। **ve detī haĩ.** *They give.*

यह देता है। **yah detā hai.** *He (this one) gives.*	यह देती है। **yah detī hai.** *She (this one) gives.*
ये देते हैं। **ye dete haĩ.** *They (these people) give.*	ये देती हैं। **ye detī haĩ.** *They (these people) give.*

And since this lesson is all about shopping, let's also look at the different forms of the verb *to shop* खरीदना **kharīdnā.**

MASCULINE	FEMININE
मैं खरीदता हूँ। **maĩ kharīdtā hū̃.** *I buy.*	मैं खरीदती हूँ। **maĩ kharīdtī hū̃.** *I buy.*
तुम खरीदते हो। **tum kharīdte ho.** *You buy.*	तुम खरीदती हो। **tum kharīdtī ho.** *You buy.*
आप खरीदते हो। **āp kharīdte ho.** *You buy.*	आप खरीदती हो। **āp kharīdtī ho.** *You buy.*
हम खरीदते हैं। **ham kharīdte haĩ.** *We buy.*	हम खरीदती हैं। **ham kharīdtī haĩ.** *We buy.*

वह खरीदता है। **vah kharīdtā hai.** *He buys.*	वह खरीदती है। **vah kharīdtī hai.** *She buys.*
वे खरीदते हैं। **ve kharīdte haĩ.** *They buy.*	वे खरीदती हैं। **ve kharīdtī haĩ.** *They buy.*
यह खरीदता है। **yah kharīdtā hai.** *He (this one) buys.*	यह खरीदती है। **yah kharīdtī hai.** *She (this one) buys.*
ये खरीदते हैं। **ye kharīdte haĩ.** *They (these people) buy.*	ये खरीदती हैं। **ye kharīdtī haĩ.** *They (these people) buy.*

Take It Further 3

8F Take It Further 3

Let's learn how to form sentences using the verbs you just learned, with both singular and plural subject pronouns, together with the word कमीज़ **kamīz** (*shirt*).

लेना LENĀ

मैं कमीज़ लेता हूँ। **maĩ kamīz letā hũ.** *I take a shirt.*	वह कमीज़ लेती है। **vah kamīz letī hai.** *She takes a shirt.*

ये कमीज़ लेते हैं। **ye kamīz lete haĩ.** *They take a shirt.*	वे कमीज़ लेती हैं। **ve kamīz lete haĩ.** *They take a shirt.*

देना DENĀ

मैं कमीज़ देता हूँ। **maĩ kamīz detā hū̃.** *I give a shirt.*	वह कमीज़ देती है। **vah kamīz detī hai.** *She gives a shirt.*
ये कमीज़ देते हैं। **ye kamīz dete haĩ.** *They give a shirt.*	वे कमीज़ देती हैं। **ve kamīz dete haĩ.** *They give a shirt.*

खरीदना KHARĪDNĀ

मैं कमीज़ खरीदता हूँ। **maĩ kamīz kharīdtā hū̃.** *I buy a shirt.*	वह कमीज़ खरीदती है। **vah kamīz kharīdtī hai.** *She buys a shirt.*
ये कमीज़ खरीदते हैं। **ye kamīz kharīdte haĩ.** *They buy a shirt.*	वे कमीज़ खरीदती हैं। **ve kamīz kharīdte haĩ.** *They buy a shirt.*

Let's also take a quick look at some plurals to revise. Remember, if there is a masculine noun with an ending in आ ā, the plural form will usually end in ए e.

कपड़ा **kapṛā** *cloth*	कपड़े **kapṛe** *clothes*
जूता **jūtā** *shoe*	जूते **jūte** *shoes*
कुर्ता **kurtā** *tunic*	कुर्ते **kurte** *tunics*
दुपट्टा **dupaṭṭā** *stole*	दुपट्टे **dupaṭṭe** *stoles*

Also remember, if the singular noun ends in a consonant, it will remain the same in plural.

कमीज़ **kamīz** *shirt*	कमीज़ **kamīz** *shirts*
बरतन **bartan** *utensils/vessels*	बरतन **bartan** *utensils/vessels*

पेड़ **peṛ** *tree*	पेड़ **peṛ** *trees*
फूल **phūl** *flower*	फूल **phūl** *flowers*

Now let's also use the plural forms in sentences. Don't worry if you can't remember all of it right now. You'll get more practice as we move along, gradually.

मैं जूते लेता हूँ। **maĩ jūte letā hū̃.** *I take shoes.*	वह जूते लेती है। **vah jūte letī hai.** *She takes shoes.*
ये कपड़े लेते हैं। **ye kapṛe lete haĩ.** *They take clothes.*	वे कपड़े लेती हैं। **ve kapṛe letī haĩ.** *They take clothes.*
मैं कुर्ते देता हूँ। **maĩ kurte detā hū̃.** *I give tunics.*	वह कुर्ते देती है। **vah kurte detī hai.** *She gives tunics.*
ये जूते देते हैं। **ye jūte dete haĩ.** *They (these people) give shoes.*	वे जूते देती हैं। **ve jūte detī haĩ.** *They give shoes.*

मैं कुर्ते खरीदता हूँ। **maĩ kurte kharīdtā hū̃.** *I buy tunics.*	वह कुर्ते खरीदती है। **vah kurte kharīdtī hai.** *She buys tunics.*
ये जूते खरीदते हैं। **ye jūte kharīdte haĩ.** *They (these people) buy shoes.*	वे जूते खरीदती हैं। **ve jūte kharīdtī haĩ.** *They buy shoes.*

Work Out 1

8G Work Out 1

Let's review what we've learned so far. Listen to your audio, and fill in the missing words. Then translate the sentences. Keep in mind the gender agreement in both plural and singular form of the adjectives, wherever they are used.

1. मेरे ________________ महंगे हैं।

   mere ________________ mahãnge haĩ.

2. उसको सस्ता ________________ चाहिए।

   usko sastā ________________ cāhiye.

3. मैं ________________ हूँ।

   maĩ ________________ hū̃.

4. यह ________________ है।

   yah ________________ hai.

5. वे ________________ हैं।

ve ________________ haĩ.

6. उनको ________________ दिखाओ।

unko ________________ dikhāo.

7. वह ________________ है।

vah ________________ hai.

ANSWER KEY

1. कपड़े **kapṛe** (*My clothes are expensive.*) 2. लहंगा **lahãngā** (*She wants a cheap skirt.*) 3. देता **detā** (*I give.*) 4. महंगा **mahãngā** (*This is expensive.*) 5. लेते **lete** (*They take.*) 6. छोटी कमीज़ **choṭī kamīz** (*Show them a small shirt.*) 7. देती **detī** (*She gives.*)

Bring It All Together

8H Bring It All Together

Let's look at some sentences.

मुझको कुछ सामान खरीदना है।
mujhko kuch sāmān kharīdnā hai.
I want to buy some stuff/things.

मुझको नीली कमीज़ दो।
mujhko nīlī kamīz do.
Give me the blue shirt.

यह बहुत बड़ा है।
yah bahut baṛā hai.
This is too large.

दूसरा दिखाओ।
dūsrā dikhāo.
Show me the other one.

नहीं, और दिखाओ।
nahī̃, aur dikhāo.
No, show me more variety.

यह महंगा है।
yah mahãngā hai.
This is expensive.

कुछ सस्ता दो।
kuch sastā do.
Give me something cheap.

मुझको यह पसंद है।
mujhko yah pasand hai.
I like this.

मुझको दुपट्टा दो।
mujhko dupaṭṭā do.
Give me a stole.

Did you recognize words from the previous lesson?

नीली कमीज़ **nīlī kamīz**	*blue shirt*

पसंद है **pasand hai**	*like*
बहुत बड़ा **bahut baṛā**	*very big*

Work Out 2

Let us now practice what you've learned so far. Fill in the blanks with the missing words.

1. नीला ________________ दिखाओ।

   nīlā ________________ dikhāo.

   Show a blue stole.

2. मुझको यह ________________ चाहिए।

   mujhko yah ________________ cāhiye.

   I want this shirt.

3. क्या ________________ है?

   kyā ________________ hai?

   What's the price?

4. यह ________________ है।

   yah ________________ hai.

   This is cheap.

5. नहीं, ______________ दिखाओ।

nahī̃, ______________ dikhāo.

No, show another.

6. उसको ______________ दिखाओ।

usko ______________ dikhāo.

Show him expensive shoes.

7. उनको ______________ दिखाओ।

unko ______________ dikhāo.

Show them clothes.

ANSWER KEY

1. दुपट्टा **dupaṭṭā** 2. कमीज़ **kamīz** 3. कीमत **kīmat** 4. सस्ता **sastā** 5. दूसरा **dūsrā** 6. महंगे जूते **mahãnge jūte** 7. कपड़े **kapṛe**

Drive It Home

Translate each phrase, using the appropriate verb form and plural.

1. *I give clothes.*

____

2. *He takes clothes.*

____

3. *They give shoes.*

____

4. *We take a piece of cloth.*

____

5. *She gives a tunic.*

6. *They take shoes.*

ANSWER KEY

1. मैं कपड़े देता हूँ। **maĩ kapṛe detā hū̃.** 2. वह कपड़े लेता है। **vah kapṛe letā hai.** 3. वे जूते देते हैं। **ve jūte dete haĩ.** 4. हम कपड़ा लेते हैं। **ham kapṛā lete haĩ.** 5. वह कुर्ता लेती है। **vah kurtā letī hai.** 6. वे जूते लेते हैं। **ve jūte lete haĩ.**

Culture Note

Bargaining for a lower price when out shopping is common in India. In most cases, people try talking storekeepers into reducing the prices of merchandise by finding some flaw in it, or choosing to try out the same thing at a competitor's. With the opening up of malls and large shopping centers in contemporary times though, this trend has seen a reduction. However, in smaller shops and independent stores, people still prefer to bargain, even if it means a difference of just a couple of tens of rupees.

As part of bargaining practices, shoppers will often ask to be shown different varieties, colors, and sizes, etc. and insist that the product is not worth its asking price. Depending on the shopping area, competition, and town size, the shopkeeper may agree to reduce the price, or politely tell them to seek out other options.

Parting Words

You've come to the end of your eighth lesson! By now you should know how to:

- ☐ Vocabulary related to shopping/buying. (Still unsure? Go back to Vocabulary Builder 1 or Vocabulary Builder 2.)
- ☐ How to express *want, take, give*, etc. when out shopping. (Still unsure? Go back to Grammar Builder 1.)
- ☐ The present imperfective. (Still unsure? Go back to Grammar Builder 2.)
- ☐ Devanagari: Group 7 & 8 consonants: श śa, ष ṣa, स sa, र ra, ड़ ṛa, ढ़ ṛha. (Still unsure? Go back to Take It Further 1.)

Word Recall

Let's review the vocabulary. Match the Hindi expressions in the left column with the English equivalents on the right.

1. दिखाओ
   dikhāo
2. क्या कीमत है?
   kyā kīmat hai?
3. दूसरा
   dūsrā
4. जूते
   jūte
5. बड़ा नाप
   baṛā nāp
6. छोटा नाप
   choṭā nāp
7. कुछ नया
   kuch nayā

a. *small size*
b. *another one*
c. *something new*
d. *large size*
e. *show*
f. *shoes*
g. *What is the price?*

ANSWER KEY

1. e; 2. g; 3. b; 4. f; 5 d; 6. a; 7. c

Lesson 9: At Work

पाठ ९: काम पर

pāṭh nau: kām par

In this lesson, you'll learn expressions and words and phrases that will help you get by at the office or workplace. You'll learn:

- □ Vocabulary related to going to work; how to say lunch, tea break, etc.
- □ Expressions for time, and more about Hindi postpositions.
- □ Days of week, names of months.
- □ Devanagari: Group 9 consonants ह ha, य ya, व va, ल la, ज़ za, फ़ fa.

Are you ready to begin?

Vocabulary Builder 1

9A Vocabulary Builder 1

दफ्तर	daphtar	*office (m.)*
रास्ता	rāstā	*route/road (m.)*
छुट्टी	chuṭṭī	*break (f.)/holiday*
समय	samay	*time (m.)*

खाने का समय	**khānē kā samay**	*time to eat*
चाय का समय	**cāy kā samay**	*time for tea (tea break)*
दोपहर	**dopahar**	*afternoon (m.)*
काम	**kām**	*work (m.)*
नौकरी	**naukrī**	*job (f.)*
नाश्ता	**nāśtā**	*breakfast (m.)*
सुबह	**subah**	*morning (f.)*
रात	**rāt**	*night (f.)*
शाम	**śām**	*evening (f.)*
लम्बी छुट्टी	**lambī chuṭṭī**	*long holiday/vacation (f.)*

Take It Further 1

9B Take It Further 1

The Hindi word for holiday is छुट्टी **chuṭṭī**. There is no separate word for saying break, lunch break, or vacations. The same word is also used when talking about leave. छुट्टी **chuṭṭī** denotes a single holiday or break, while the word छुट्टियाँ **chuṭṭiyā̃** is the plural form, and is also used when talking about a vacation, summer holidays, etc.

Other words or adjectives are added to describe the break/ holiday/vacation. Naturally, postpositions are used in this kind of construction. And because छुट्टी

chuṭṭī is a feminine noun, it retains its form even in the oblique case. Remember that feminine singular nouns are identical in both, nominative and oblique forms.

गर्मी की छुट्टियाँ	garmī kī chuṭṭiyā̃	*summer holidays*
दोपहर की छुट्टी	dopahar kī chuṭṭī	*afternoon break*
एक दिन की छुट्टी	ek din kī chuṭṭī	*a day off*

Vocabulary Practice 1

Let's practice the vocabulary that you've learned. Match the Hindi in the first column to the English equivalent in the second.

1. नाश्ता nāśtā	a. *office*
2. चाय का समय cāy kā samay	b. *evening*
3. शाम śām	c. *breakfast*
4. दफ्तर daphtar	d. *work*
5. काम kām	e. *time for tea*

6. नौकरी

   naukrī

7. लम्बी छुट्टी

   lambī chuṭṭī

f. *long holiday/vacation*

g. *job*

ANSWER KEY

1. c; 2. e; 3. b; 4. a; 5. d; 6. g; 7. f

Grammar Builder 1

9C Grammar Builder 1

Let's look at some expressions for describing time periods.

कितने बजे?	**kitne baje?**	*At what time?*
आज	**āj**	*today*
कल	**kal**	*tomorrow*
रोज़	**roz**	*every day*
अभी	**abhī**	*right now*
कब?	**kab?**	*when?*

The term बजे **baje** is a form of the verb बजना **bajnā**, which literally means *to ring.* The term बजे **baje** indicates time in plural. When talking about singular, (*one o'clock*) बजे **baje** changes to बजा **bajā**.

एक बजा है।	**ek bajā hai.**	*It's one o'clock.*

We will look at how to tell time in greater detail ahead, in Grammar Builder 2.

Now let's look at some examples using the vocabulary you just learned.

आपकी छुट्टी कब है?	**āpkī chuṭṭī kab hai?**	*When is your vacation?*
मैं रोज़ खेलता हूँ।	**maĩ roz kheltā hũ**	*I play every day.*
कल छुट्टी है।	**kal chuṭṭī hai.**	*Tomorrow is a holiday.*
अभी चाय का समय है।	**abhī cāy kā samay hai.**	*It's time for tea right now.*
दफ्तर कितने बजे है?	**daphtar kitne baje hai?**	*What time is work?* *(lit.: What time is office?)*

Take It Further 2

9D Take It Further 2

MORE ON POSTPOSITIONS

Let's take a closer look at Hindi postpositions. You remember being introduced to postpositions in Lesson 6: Describing Things. Let's review them in the context of the workplace.

में mẽ *in/around*	मैं दफ्तर में हूँ।	maĩ daphtar mẽ hū̃.	*I'm in the office.*
	वह स्कूल में है।	vah skūl mẽ hai.	*He is in school.*
पर par *on/at*	मैं छुट्टी पर हूँ।	maĩ chuṭṭī par hū̃.	*I'm on vacation.*
	वह दुपहर की छुट्टी पर है।	vah dupahar kī chuṭṭī par hai.	*She is on a lunch break.*
से se *from*	दफ्तर से	daphtar se	*from the office*
	घर से	ghar se	*from home*
तक tak *up to/until*	रात तक	rāt tak	*until night*
	दिल्ली तक	dillī tak	*up to Delhi*
का kā *of/for (indicates belonging)*	दफ्तर का समय	daphtar kā samay	*time for work*
	नाश्ते का समय।	nāśte kā samay	*time for breakfast*

Remember that nouns before the postposition are in oblique case. The oblique case becomes apparent in masculine singular nouns ending in the vowel आ ā when it takes the ending ए e. Let's look at some constructions using nouns familiar to you.

NOMINATIVE	OBLIQUE	
चौराहा caurāha *intersection*	चौराहे caurāhe	चौराहे से बाए caurāhe se bayẽ *left at the intersection*
रास्ता rāstā *road*	रास्ते rāste	रास्ते से सीध rāste se sīdhe *straight ahead from the road*
सस्ता sastā *cheap*	सस्ते saste	सस्ते में दो saste mẽ do *give it cheap (give it for a lesser price)*
दरवाज़ा darvāzā *door*	दरवाज़े darvāze	दरवाज़े से दूर darvāze se dūr *far from the door/ some distance away from the door*

More About the Postposition का kā

The postposition का kā changes form depending on the gender and number of the noun it is modifying.

M. SINGULAR NOUN	F. SINGULAR NOUN	M. PLURAL NOUN	F. PLURAL NOUN
दरवाज़ा **darvāzā** *door*	सब्ज़ी **sabzī** *vegetable*	दरवाज़े **darvāze** *doors*	सब्ज़ियाँ **sabziyā̃** *vegetables*
का **kā**	की **kī**	के **ke**	की **kī**
का दरवाज़ा **kā darvāzā**	की सब्ज़ी **kī sabzī**	के दरवाज़े **ke darvāze**	की सब्ज़ियाँ **kī sabziyā̃**
लकड़ी का दरवाज़ा **lakṛī kā darvāzā** *wooden door* *(door of wood)*	सलाद की सब्ज़ी **salād kī sabzī** *vegetable for salad*	लकड़ी के दरवाज़े **lakṛī ke darvāze** *wooden doors* *(doors of wood)*	सलाद की सब्ज़ियाँ **salād kī sabziyā̃** *vegetables for salad*

Take It Further 3

At this point, turn to your *Guide to Reading and Writing Hindi*, and cover:

☐ Group 9 Consonants: ह **ha** , य **ya** , व **va**, ल **la**, ज़ **za**, फ़ **fa**

Vocabulary Builder 2

9E Vocabulary Builder 2

दिन	**din**	*day (m.)*
सोमवार	**somvār**	*Monday (m.)*
मंगलवार	**mangalvār**	*Tuesday (m.)*
बुधवार	**budhvār**	*Wednesday (m.)*
गुरुवार	**guruvār**	*Thursday (m.)*
शुक्रवार	**śukravār**	*Friday (m.)*
शनिवार	**śanivār**	*Saturday (m.)*
रविवार	**ravivār**	*Sunday (m.)*
कभी कभी	**kabhī kabhī**	*sometimes*
हमेशा	**hameśā**	*always*
कभी नहीं	**kabhī nahī̃**	*never*
जल्दी	**jaldī**	*quick*
सिर्फ	**sirph**	*only*
हफ्ता	**haphtā**	*week (m.)*
घंटा	**ghanṭā**	*hour (m.)*

Vocabulary Practice 2

Match the following English terms with their Hindi equivalents.

1. *sometimes*	a. जल्दी **jaldī**
2. *never*	b. सोमवार **somvār**
3. *Monday*	c. कभी कभी **kabhī kabhī**
4. *quick*	d. हमेशा **hameśā**
5. *Thursday*	e. घंटा **ghaṇṭā**
6. *hour*	f. कभी नहीं **kabhī nahī̃**
7. *always*	g. गुरुवार **guruvār**

ANSWER KEY

1. c; 2. f; 3. b; 4. a; 5. g; 6. e; 7. d

Grammar Builder 2

9F Grammar Builder 2

TALKING ABOUT DAYS OF THE WEEK

When talking about the days of the week in Hindi, you will use a lot of postpositions. To express that something happens on a particular date, the postposition को **ko** is used; corresponding in this case to the English "on."

सोमवार को **somvār ko**	*on Monday*
हमेशा रविवार को **hameśā ravivār ko**	*always on Sunday*
कभी कभी शुक्रवार को **kabhī kabhī śukravār ko**	*sometimes on Friday*

Look at how other postpositions are used:

मैं सोमवार से शनिवार तक काम करता हूँ। **maĩ somvār se śanivār tak kām kartā hũ.**	*I work from Monday to Saturday.*
वह सात घंटे काम करती है। **vah sāt ghaṇṭe kām kartī hai.**	*She works for seven hours.*

सिर्फ बुधवार को **sirph budhvār ko**	*only on Wednesday*
शाम को **śām ko**	*in the evening*
हफ्ते में एक बार **haphte mẽ ek bār**	*once a week*

Dates

Different regions in India follow different traditional calendars. Thus, almost every region has its own separate New Year day celebration and auspicious observances. However, the calendar followed for business and everyday purposes is the Gregorian one. Here are the months of the year.

जनवरी **janvarī** *January*	फरवरी **pharvarī** *February*	मार्च **mārc** *March*
अप्रैल **aprail** *April*	मई **maī** *May*	जून **jūn** *June*
जुलाई **julāī** *July*	अगस्त **agast** *August*	सितम्बर **sitambar** *September*

अक्तूबर **aktūbar** *October*	नवम्बर **navambar** *November*	दिसम्बर **disambar** *December*

क्या तारीख है?	**kyā tārīkh hai?**	*What date is it?*

There are different ways to express a date तारीख **tārīkh**. Note the postpositions.

१६ मई **solah maī**	*16 May*
१६ मई को **solah maī ko**	*on 16 May*
मई के महीने में **maī ke mahīne mẽ**	*in the month of May*

Telling Time

There are a number of ways to ask, *What time is it?* in Hindi. Let's look at the most common one.

कितने बजे हैं?	**kitne baje haĩ?**	*What time is it?*

To answer in Hindi, use the word बजे **baje** with numbers.

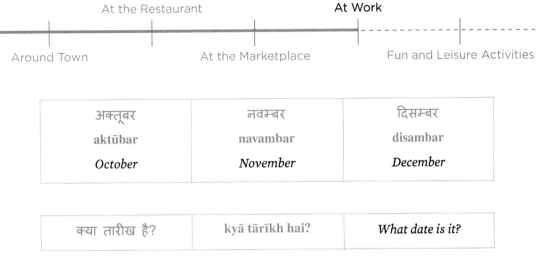

४ बजे हैं	**cār baje haĩ**	*It's 4 o'clock*
१ बजा है	**ek baja hai**	*It's 1 o'clock*

Note that 1 is singular, hence the verb है will not be nasalized. When talking about time in terms of hours and minutes, use the word बजकर **bajkar**, followed by the number of minutes.

चार बजकर तीस मिनिट **cār bajkar tīs minit**	*4:30*
तीन बजकर सात मिनिट **tīn bajkar sāt minit**	*3:07*
पांच बजे हैं। **pā̃c baje haĩ.**	*The time is 5.*
चार बजकर तीस मिनिट हैं। **cār bajkar tīs minit haĩ.**	*The time is 4:30.*
तीन बजकर सात मिनिट। **tīn bajkar sāt minit.**	*(The time is) 3:07.*

Note that the verb has been dropped in the last example. This is a more commonly used form.

Now let's look at a few sentences telling time. Note the postpositions.

तीन बजकर तीस मिनिट पर **tīn bajkar tīs minit par**	*at 3:30*
शाम के पांच बजकर दस मिनिट हैं। **śām ke pā̃c bajkar das minit haĩ.**	*It's 5:10 in the evening.*
सुबह के सात बजे **subah ke sāt baje**	*at 7 in the morning*
दोपहर के दो बजे **dopahar ke do baje**	*at 2 in the afternoon*

You don't need postpositions when describing something taking place at a particular hour.

दफ्तर नौ बजे हैं। **daphtar nau baje haĩ.**	*Work is at 9.*
खाने का समय दो बजे ह। **khāne ka samay do baje hai.**	*Lunch time is 2 o'clock.*

Take It Further 4

9G Take It Further 4

Let's look at the Hindi equivalents of the words *Quarter* and *Half past.*

सवा savā	*quarter past*	सवा दो बजे हैं। savā do baje haĩ.	*It's quarter past two. (2:15)*
पौने paune	*quarter to*	पौने नौ बजे हैं। paune nau baje haĩ.	*It's quarter to nine. (8:45)*
साढ़े sāṛhe	*half past*	साढ़े नौ बजे हैं। sāṛhe nau baje haĩ.	*It's half past nine. (9:30)*
डेढ़ ḍeṛh	*half past one*	डेढ़ बजे हैं। ḍeṛh baje haĩ.	*It's half past one. (1:30)*
ढाई ḍhāī	*half past two*	ढाई बजे हैं। ḍhāī baje haĩ.	*It's half past two. (2:30)*

Note the two unique constructions for *half past one* and *half past two.*

Work Out 1

9H Work Out 1

Let's go over everything that you've learned so far. Listen to your audio and fill in the blanks with the words that you hear.

1. ________________ के सात बजे हैं।

________________ ke sāt baje haĩ.

It's 7 in the evening.

2. तीस ________________

tīs ________________

30 November

3. छुट्टियाँ ________________ अप्रैल से हैं।

chuṭṭiyā̃ ________________ aprail se haĩ.

Vacation is from April 30.

4. ________________ का खाना दो बजे है।

________________ kā khānā do baje hai.

Lunch is at 2 in the afternoon.

5. स्कूल की छुट्टी ________________ दस से है।

skūl kī chuṭṭī ________________ das se hai.

School break is from September 10.

6. ________________ क्या है?

________________ kyā hai?

What is the time?

7. ________________ क्या है?

________________ kyā hai?

What is the date?

ANSWER KEY

1. शाम śām 2. नवम्बर navambar 3. तीस tīs 4. दोपहर dopahar 5. सितम्बर sitambar 6. समय samay 7. तारीख tārīkh

Bring It All Together

91 Bring It All Together

Now let's listen to a monologue. Note the descriptions.

यह मेरी स्कुल है।

yah merī skūl hai.

This is my school.

मैं शिक्षक हूँ।

maĩ śikṣak hū̃.

I am a teacher.

स्कुल का समय सुबह १० बजे से शाम ४ बजे तक का है।

skūl kā samay subah das baje se śām cār baje tak kā hai.

School hours are from 10am to 4pm.

स्कूल बाज़ार के पास है।

skūl bāzār ke pās hai.

The school is near the market.

खाने के समय एक छोटा अवकाश मिलता है।

khāne ke samay ek chotā avkāś miltā hai.

There is a short lunch break.

मेरी मई के महीने में लम्बी छुट्टी है।

merī maī ke mahīne mẽ lambī chuṭṭī hai.

I have a vacation in the month of May.

मेरी पत्नी रूपा वकील है।
merī patnī rūpa vakīl hai.
My wife Rupa is a lawyer.

वह उसका दफ्तर है, चौराहे के पास।
vah uskā daphtar hai, caurāhe ke pās.
That is her office, near the intersection.

अभी शाम के ४ बजे हैं।
abhī śām ke cār baje haĩ.
It's 4 in the evening now.

दफ्तर में यह चाय का समय है।
daphtar mẽ yah cāy ka samay hai.
This is tea time at the office.

अच्छा। फिर मिलेंगे!
acchā. phir milenge!
Okay. See you later!

Did you notice a new word अवकाश **avkāś**? It is another word for *break* or *interlude* or *recess*. It can also mean *holiday* and *vacation*, but the usage is not very common.

Work Out 2

Now let's practice what you've learned so far. Fill in the blanks with the missing words.

1. माफ कीजिए, आपका ________________ कितने बजे है?

   māf kījiye, āpkā ________________ kitne baje hai?

   Excuse me, what time is work (office)?

2. वह दफ्तर में ________________ करती है।

   vah daphtar mẽ ________________ kartī hai.

   She works in an office.

3. दफ्तर का ________________ सुबह आठ बजे से शाम चार बजे तक है।

   daphtar kā ________________ subah āṭh baje se śām cār baje tak hai.

   Office hours are 8am to 4pm.

4. तारीख ________________ तीस है।

   tārīkh ________________ tīs hai.

   The date is November 30.

5. ________________ एक लम्बा अवकाश मिलता है।

   ________________ ek lambā avkāś miltā hai.

   There is a long lunch break (lunch time).

6. मैं ________________ काम करता हूँ।

   maĩ ________________ kām karta hũ.

   I work in the morning.

7. सब लोग ________________ हैं।

   sab log ________________ haĩ.

   Everyone is busy.

ANSWER KEY

1. दफ्तर **daphtar** 2. काम **kām** 3. समय **samay** 4. नवम्बर **navambar** 5. खाने के समय **khāne ke samay** 6. सुबह **subah** 7. व्यस्त **vyast**

Drive It Home

Let's practice telling the time and date. Translate into Hindi.

1. *9:30* ________________
2. *8:10* ________________
3. *June 17* ________________
4. *September 24* ________________
5. *9 o'clock in the morning* ________________
6. *at 6:30* ________________
7. *from 5:10* ________________

ANSWER KEY

1. नौ बजकर तीस मिनिट nau bajkar tīs minit 2. आठ बजकर दस मिनिट āṭh bajkar das minit 3. सत्रह जून satraha jūn 4. सितम्बर चौबीस sitambar caubīs 5. सुबह के नौ बजे subah ke nau baje 6. छह बजकर तीस मिनिट chah bajkar tīs minit par 7. पांच बजकर दस मिनिट से pā̃c bajkar das minit se

Parting Words

बधाई! badhāī! *Congratulations!* You've come to the end of your ninth lesson! By now you should know:

- ☐ Vocabulary related to going to work; how to say *lunch, tea break,* etc. (Still unsure? Go back to Vocabulary Builder 1.)
- ☐ Expressions for time, and more about Hindi postpositions. (Still unsure? Go back to Grammar Builder 1 or Take It Further 2.)

☐ Days of week, names of months. (Still unsure? Go back to Grammar Builder 2.)

☐ Devanagari: Group 9 alphabets ह ha, य ya, व va, ल la, ज़ za, फ fa. (Still unsure? Go back to Take It Further 3.)

Word Recall

Let's review the most important vocabulary you learned in Lesson 9. Match the Hindi in the first column with the English equivalents in the second column.

1. कभी नहीं **kabhī nahī̃**	a. *afternoon*
2. महीना **mahīnā**	b. *sometimes*
3. कभी कभी **kabhī kabhī**	c. *never*
4. समय **samay**	d. *January*
5. जनवरी **janvarī**	e. *month*
6. हमेशा **hameśā**	f. *date*
7. तारीख **tārīkh**	g. *time*
8. दोपहर **dopahar**	h. *always*

ANSWER KEY

1. c; 2. e; 3. b; 4. g; 5. d; 6. h; 7. f; 8. a

Lesson 10: Fun and Leisure Activities

पाठ १०: आराम और मनोरंजन

pāṭh das: ārām aur manoranjan

This tenth lesson is all about fun and leisure. You'll learn:

- ☐ Expressions and vocabulary related to leisure and fun activities.
- ☐ More verbs in the present imperfective and Conjunct verbs.
- ☐ Expressing *like* and *love:* पसंद/बहुत पसंद **pasand/bahut pasand**.
- ☐ Devanagari: Halant and conjunct characters.

Are you ready to begin?

Vocabulary Builder 1

▶ 10A Vocabulary Builder 1

खेलना	**khelnā**	*to play*
टीवी देखना	**ṭīvī dekhnā**	*to watch TV*
टहलना	**ṭahalnā**	*to walk (for leisure)*

सैर करना	**sair karnā**	*to go on an outing/ excursion/to go sightseeing*
सिनेमा देखना	**sinemā dekhnā**	*to watch movies*
दोस्तों को मिलना	**dostõ ko milnā**	*to visit friends*
साथ-साथ	**sāth-sāth**	*together*
दावत	**dāvat**	*feast (f.)*
तैरना	**tairnā**	*swimming (m.)*
दिन भर	**din bhar**	*all day*
चलो चलें	**calo calẽ**	*let's go*

Vocabulary Practice 1

Let's practice the vocabulary that you've learned. Match the Hindi in the first column to the English equivalent in the second.

1. सिनेमा देखना
   sinemā dekhnā
2. दोस्तों को मिलना
   dostõ ko milnā
3. टीवी देखना
   ṭīvī dekhnā

a. *to visit friends*

b. *together*

c. *feast*

4. साथ-साथ
sāth-sāth

5. खेलना
khelnā

6. टहलना
ṭahalnā

7. सैर करना
sair karnā

8. दावत
dāvat

d. *to watch movies*

e. *to walk (for leisure)*

f. *to play*

g. *to watch TV*

h. *to go on an outing/excursion*

ANSWER KEY

1. d; 2. a; 3. g; 4. b; 5. f; 6. e; 7. h; 8. c

Grammar Builder 1

10B Grammar Builder 1

MORE VERBS IN THE PRESENT IMPERFECTIVE

Let's look at some simple sentences and constructions that you can use while talking about leisure activities. Remember the postpositions you learned? We will revise them as well. To form the present imperfective, remember you need the appropriate imperfective participles. Let's look at some common verbs and their imperfective participles.

INFINITIVE	M. SINGULAR	F. SINGULAR	M. PLURAL	F. PLURAL
खेलना **khelnā** *to play*	खेलता **kheltā**	खेलती **kheltī**	खेलते **khelte**	खेलती **kheltī**
टहलना **ṭahalnā** *to walk*	टहलता **ṭahaltā**	टहलती **ṭahaltī**	टहलते **ṭahalte**	टहलती **ṭahaltī**
करना **karnā** *to do*	करता **kartā**	करती **kartī**	करते **karte**	करती **kartī**
देना **denā** *to give*	देता **detā**	देती **detī**	देते **dete**	देती **detī**
जाना **jānā** *to go*	जाता **jātā**	जाती **jātī**	जाते **jāte**	जाती **jātī**
तैरना **tairnā** *to swim*	तैरता **tairtā**	तैरती **tairtī**	तैरते **tairte**	तैरती **tairtī**
देखना **dekhnā** *to watch*	देखता **dekhtā**	देखती **dekhtī**	देखते **dekhte**	देखती **dekhtī**

रहना **rahanā** *to stay*	रहता **rahatā**	रहती **rahatī**	रहते **rahate**	रहती **rahatī**

Let's look at some examples.

मैं सिनेमा देखती हूँ।	**maĩ sinemā dekhtī hū̃.**	*I (f.) watch a movie.*
हम साथ साथ खेलते हैं।	**ham sāth sāth khelte haĩ.**	*We play together.*
वे टीवी देखते हैं।	**ve ṭīvī dekhte haĩ.**	*They (m.) watch TV.*
वह तैरता है।	**vah tairtā hai.**	*He swims.*

Conjunct Verbs

Hindi has a lot of verbs that consist of two components—that is, a verb along with a noun or an adjective, for example, सैर **sair** (*outing*), and आराम **ārām** (*rest*) are combined with the verb करना **karnā** (*to do*) to express a compound action. These are called conjunct verbs; and usually the main verb in these combinations is करना **karnā** (*to do*).

मैं आराम करती हूँ।	**maĩ ārām kartī hū̃.**	*I rest. (lit.: I do rest) (f.)*
हम सैर करते हैं।	**ham sair karte haĩ.**	*We go on an excursion. (lit.: We do an excursion.)*
वह आराम करता है।	**vah ārām karta hai.**	*He rests.*

वे सैर करते हैं।	ve sair karte haĩ.	*They go on an excursion. (lit.: They do an excursion.)*
मैं तैरती हूँ।	maĩ sair kartī hũ.	*I swim. (f.)*

Let's also look at a few sentences using the phrase चलो calo (*come/come along/ let's go*). This is the imperative form of the verb चलना calnā (*to walk*).

चलो, आराम करते हैं।	calo, ārām karte haĩ.	*Come, let's take rest.*
चलो, खेलते हैं।	calo, khelte haĩ.	*Come, let's play.*
चलो, टीवी देखते हैं।	calo, ṭīvī dekhte haĩ.	*Come, let's watch TV.*
चलो, टहलते हैं।	calo, ṭahalte haĩ.	*Come, let's take a walk.*

Take It Further 1

Let's take a closer look at Devanagari now. Turn to the *Guide to Reading and Writing Hindi* and cover:

☐ Group 10 alphabets: Halant and Conjunct characters

Vocabulary Builder 2

10C Vocabulary Builder 2

कल छुट्टी है।	**kal chuṭṭī hai.**	*Tomorrow's a holiday.*
सिनेमा देखते हैं।	**sinemā dekhte haĩ.**	*Let's go to the cinema. (Let's 'watch' the cinema.)*
तुमको तैरना आता है?	**tumko tairnā ātā hai?**	*Do you know how to swim?*
किधर जाना है?	**kidhar jānā hai?**	*Where do (you) want to go?*
कुछ खेलते हैं।	**kuch khelte haĩ.**	*Let's play something.*
कौन सी फिल्म लगी है?	**kaun sī philm lagī hai?**	*Which film is on?*
छुट्टी के दिन	**chuṭṭī ke din**	*on vacation/on an off-day (lit.: on the day of leave)*
शौक	**śauk**	*hobby (m.) (interest)*
तुम्हारे क्या शौक है?	**tumhāre kyā śauk hai?**	*What are your hobbies?*
कोई नई जगह।	**koī nayī jagah.**	*some new place*
हम सब	**ham sab.**	*all of us*

Note that the word for hobby शौक **śauk**, remains the same, both singular and plural forms.

Vocabulary Practice 2

Match the English expressions on the left with the Hindi equivalents on the right.

1. *Which film is on?*
2. *Let's play something.*
3. *Watch a movie.*
4. *Do you know how to swim?*
5. *Is there a new place?*
6. *Tomorrow is a holiday.*
7. *Where do you want to go?*

a. सिनेमा देखते हैं।
sinemā dekhte haĩ.

b. कोई नई जगह है?
koī nayī jagah hai?

c. कौन सी फिल्म लगी है?
kaun sī philm lagī hai?

d. किधर जाना है?
kidhar jānā hai?

e. कल छुट्टी है।
kal chuṭṭī hai.

f. तुमको तैरना आता है?
tumko tairnā ātā hai?

g. कुछ खेलते हैं।
kuch khelte haĩ.

ANSWER KEY

1. c; 2 g; 3. a; 4. f; 5. b; 6. e; 7. d

Take It Further 2

10D Take It Further 2

In Hindi, pronouns like हम (*us/we*) are often implied in conversations, and not necessarily stated. You have already seen this in the vocabulary. Let's take a closer look at this construction.

कुछ खेलते हैं।

kuch khelte haĩ.

(Let's) play something.

किधर जाना है?

kidhar jānā hai?

Where do (you) want to go?

Grammar Builder 2

10E Grammar Builder 2

EXPRESSING *LIKE*, *LOVE*, *WANT TO*, AND *DON'T WANT TO*

In Hindi, there isn't an equivalent of the verb *love*. Instead, it is expressed by adding the term बहुत **bahut** (*very/more*) to the sentence, before the word पसंद **pasand** (*like*).

You have already seen different usages of पसंद **pasand** in the Lesson 7: At the Restaurant. We will now look at it more closely.

मुझको खेलना पसंद है।	**mujhko khelnā pasand hai.**	*I like to play.*
मुझको खेलना बहुत पसंद है।	**mujhko khelnā bahut pasand hai.**	*I love to play.*
उसको तैरना पसंद है।	**usko tairnā pasand hai.**	*She/he likes to swim.*
हमको तैरना बहुत पसंद है।	**hamko tairnā bahut pasand hai.**	*We love to swim.*
इनको तैरना बहुत पसंद है।	**inko tairnā bahut pasand ai.**	*They (these people) love to swim.*

Here, the verbs खेलना (*to play*) and तैरना (*to swim*) are used in their infinitive form. Let's also look at some examples.

मुझको तैरना पसंद है।	**mujhko tairnā pasand hai.**	*I like to swim.*
उसको टीवी देखना बहुत पसंद है।	**usko ṭīvī dekhnā bahut pasand hai.**	*She loves to watch TV.*
मेरे परिवार को टहलना बहुत पसंद है।	**mere parivār ko ṭahalnā bahut pasand hai.**	*My family loves to take walks.*
हम सबको दावत पसंद हैं।	**ham sabko dāvat pasand haĩ.**	*All of us love feasts.*
उसको खेलना पसंद है।	**usko khelnā pasand hai.**	*He likes to play.*

Let's look at the word चाहिए **cāhiye** once again. In Lesson 7 you saw it used to express want:

उनको पानी चाहिए।	**unko pānī cāhiye.**	*They want water.*
मुझको रोटी चाहिए।	**mujhko roṭī cāhiye.**	*I want a roti.*
हमको जगह चाहिए।	**hamko jagah cāhiye.**	*We want a place (to sit).*
मुझको छुट्टी चाहिए।	**mujhko chuṭṭī cāhiye.**	*I want leave. (I want a holiday.)*
उनको दावत चाहिए।	**unko dāvat cāhiye.**	*They want a feast.*
हमको लम्बी छुट्टी चाहिए।	**hamko lambī chuṭṭī cāhiye.**	*We want a long vacation.*

Now let's look at negation. How do you say *don't want*? Simply add नहीं **nahī̃** *no* before चाहिए **cāhiye**.

मुझको छुट्टी नहीं चाहिए।	**mujhko chuṭṭī nahī̃ cāhiye.**	*I don't want a leave. (I don't want a vacation.)*
उनको दावत नहीं चाहिए।	**unko dāvat nahī̃ cāhiye.**	*They don't want a feast.*
हमको लम्बी छुट्टी नहीं चाहिए।	**hamko lambī chuṭṭī nahī̃ cāhiye.**	*We don't want a long vacation.*

Work Out 1

10F Work Out 1

Let's review what we've learned so far. Listen to your audio, and fill in the missing words. Then translate the sentences.

1. उसको टीवी देखना ________________ है।

   usko ṭīvī dekhnā ________________ hai.

   ____

2. कौन सी ________________ लगी है?

   kaun sī ________________ lagī hai?

   ____

3. कल ________________ है।

   kal ________________ hai.

   ____

4. हम सबको ________________ पसंद हैं।

   ham sabko ________________ pasand haĩ.

   ____

5. वे ________________ हैं।

   ve ________________ haĩ.

   ____

6. चलो, ________________ देखते हैं।

   calo, ________________ dekhte haĩ.

   ____

7. हम सब ______________ हैं।

ham sab ______________ haĩ.

ANSWER KEY

1. बहुत पसंद **bahut pasand** (*He loves watching TV.*) 2. फिल्म **philm** (*Which film is on?*) 3. छुट्टी **chuṭṭī** (*Tomorrow is a holiday.*) 4. दावत **dāvat** (*All of us love feasts.*) 5. सिनेमा देखते **sinemā dekhte** (*They watch a movie.*) 6. टीवी **ṭīvī** (*Come, let's watch TV.*) 7. तैरते **tairte** (*All of us swim.*)

Bring It All Together

10G Bring It All Together

Now let's listen in as siblings in a family talk about some fun and leisure activities.

कल रविवार है। छुट्टी का दिन।	**kal ravivār hai. chuṭṭī kā din.**	*Tomorrow is Sunday. It's a holiday.*
सबको रविवार बहुत पसंद है।	**sabko ravivār bahut pasand hai.**	*Everybody loves Sundays.*
हम रविवार को आराम करते हैं।	**ham ravivār ko ārām karte haĩ.**	*We rest on Sunday.*
मेरी बहन सीमा सुबह सुबह तैरने जाती है।	**merī bahan sīma subah subah tairne jātī hai.**	*My sister Seema goes for a swim in the morning.*
मेरा भाई अजय रविवार को दोपहर तक क्रिकेट खेलता है।	**merā bhāī ajay ravivār ko dopahar tak kriket̤ kheltā hai.**	*My brother Ajay plays cricket until the afternoon on Sundays.*

वह अच्छा बल्लेबाज़ है।	**vah acchā ballebāz hai.**	*He is a good batsman.*
उसका अच्छा अभ्यास भी होता है।	**uska acchā abhyās bhī hota hai.**	*He gets good practice as well.*
शाम को मेरा परिवार टीवी पर फिल्म देखता है।	**śām ko merā parivār ṭīvī par philm dekhtā hai.**	*In the evenings, my family watches a movie on the TV.*
(रविवार को) रात का खाना हम बाहर खाते हैं।	**(ravivār ko) rāt kā khānā ham bāhar khāte haĩ.**	*We eat dinner outside (on Sundays).*
तुम रविवार को क्या करते हो?	**tum ravivār ko kyā karte ho?**	*What do you do on Sundays?*

Work Out 2

Let us now practice what you've learned so far. Translate the following into Hindi.

1. *We eat dinner outside.*

2. *She likes excursions.*

3. *My family watches movies.*

4. *Today is a feast.*

5. *I rest.*

6. *I swim.*

7. *I love to play.*

ANSWER KEY

1. हम रात का खाना बाहर खाते हैं। **ham rāt kā khānā bāhar khāte haĩ.** 2. उसको सैर करना पसंद है। **usko sair karnā pasand hai.** 3. मेरा परिवार सिनेमा देखता है। **merā parivār cinemā dekhtā hai.** 4. आज दावत है। **āj dāvat hai.** 5. मैं आराम करता हूँ। **maĩ ārām kartā hũ.** 6. मैं तैरता हूँ। **maĩ tairtā hũ.** 7. मुझको खेलना बहुत पसंद है। **mujhko khelnā bahut pasand hai.**

Drive It Home

Now, let's practice possessives. Translate the following expressions into Hindi.

1. *We all love to play./All of us love to play.*

2. *I like to swim.*

3. *There's a feast today.*

4. *We have a holiday tomorrow.*

5. *Let's go out together.*

ANSWER KEY

1. हम सबको खेलना बहुत पसंद है। **ham sabko khelnā bahut pasand hai.** 2. मुझको तैरना पसंद है। **mujhko tairna pasand hai.** 3. आज दावत है। **āj dāvat hai.** 4. कल छुट्टी है। **kal chuṭṭī hai.** 5. चलो, साथ-साथ सैर करते हैं। **calo, sāth-sāth sair karte haĩ.**

Culture Note

Most companies and schools in India follow either a five and a half day or six day work week. If it is a six day work week, alternate Saturdays may be given off. In either case, Sunday remains a special day for the family, and is usually reserved for leisure activities with family and friends.

Apart from weekend chores like shopping, families with little children may plan to visit the city zoos or public parks. This becomes a good opportunity for the family to step out together. The weekend is a good time to eat out, unless something special is planned or guests are visiting.

With the advent of malls in most big cities, families may combine the activities of shopping, entertainment (such as movies) and eating out. A rising concern has been a visible reduction in children indulging in sports and physical activities. This is often attributed to changing lifestyles and children preferring sedentary activities.

Parting Words

You've come to the end of your second lesson! By now you should know:

- ☐ Expressions and vocabulary related to leisure and fun activities. (Still unsure? Go back to Vocabulary Builder 1.)
- ☐ More verbs in the present imperfective and Conjunct verbs. (Still unsure? Go back to Grammar Builder 1.)
- ☐ Expressing *like* and *love*: पसंद **pasand**/बहुत पसंद **bahut pasand**. (Still unsure? Go back to Grammar Builder 2.)
- ☐ Devanagari: Halant and conjunct characters. (Still unsure? Go back to Take It Further 1.)

Word Recall

Let's review the vocabulary together with correct possessives. Match the Hindi expressions in the left column with the English equivalents in the right column.

1. सिनेमा देखना
   sinemā dekhnā
2. दिन भर
   din bhar
3. चलो चलें
   calo calẽ
4. दोस्तों को मिलना
   dostõ ko milnā
5. खेलना
   khelnā
6. सैर करना
   sair karnā
7. टहलना
   ṭahalnā

a. *let's go*

b. *to watch movies*

c. *to walk (for leisure)*

d. *all day*

e. *to go on an outing/excursion/ sightseeing trip*

f. *to visit friends*

g. *to play*

ANSWER KEY

1. b; 2. d; 3. a; 4. f; 5 g; 6. e; 7. c

Quiz 2

Now let's review! In this section, you'll find a final quiz testing what you've learned in Lessons 1–10. Once you've completed it, score yourself to see how well you've done. If you find that you need to go back and review, please do so before continuing on to the Review Dialogues and comprehension questions.

A. Provide the Hindi equivalents for the following terms.

1. *store* ______________________
2. *road* ______________________
3. *turn right* ______________________
4. *behind* ______________________
5. *want* ______________________
6. *vegetarian* ______________________
7. *quickly* ______________________
8. *expensive* ______________________
9. *shirt* ______________________
10. *holiday* ______________________

B. Translate the following expressions using the appropriate postpositions, including compound postpositions.

1. *at the turn* ______________________
2. *ahead of the school* ______________________

3. *up to the hotel* ______________________

4. *at the river* ______________________

5. *from the road* ______________________

6. *in the city* ______________________

7. *from the post office* ______________________

8. *near the bridge* ______________________

9. *behind the post office* ______________________

10. *till there* ______________________

C. Match the Hindi expressions on the left with the English equivalents on the right.

1. दोस्तों को मिलना **dostõ ko milnā**	a. *I rest*
2. चाय का समय **cāy kā samay**	b. *Where do (you) want to go?*
3. आप क्या खाओगे? **āp kyā khāoge?**	c. *It's one o'clock.*
4. मैं तैरता हूँ। **maĩ tairtā hũ.**	d. *This (dish of) vegetable is delicious.*
5. दोपहर की छुट्टी **dopahar kī chuṭṭī**	e. *to meet friends*

6. एक बजा है।
ek bajā hai.

7. मैं आराम करता हूँ।
maĩ ārām kartā hū̃.

8. किधर जाना है?
kidhar jānā hai?

9. साथ-साथ
sāth-sāth

10. यह सब्ज़ी स्वादिष्ट है।
yah sabzī swādishṭ hai.

f. *together*

g. *tea time*

h. *afternoon break*

i. *What will you eat?*

j. *I swim.*

D. Fill in the blanks below with the appropriate adjectives or forms of verbs. Keep track of the gender while doing so.

1. यह ____________________ तीखा है।
yah ____________________ tīkhā hai.
This is more spicy.

2. वे शनिवार को ____________________ हैं।
ve śanivār ko ____________________ haĩ.
They swim on Saturdays.

3. ____________________ मंगलवार को।
____________________ mangalvār ko
always on Tuesday

4. क्या ________________ है?

kyā ________________ hai?

What's the date?

5. सुबह के ________________ हैं।

subah ke ________________ haĩ.

It's seven in the morning.

6. खाने का समय ________________ है।

khāne ka samay ________________ hai.

Lunch time is 1.30.

7. हमको ________________ चाहिए।

hamko ________________ cāhiye.

We want a bigger table.

8. वे टीवी ________________ हैं।

ve tīvī ________________ haĩ.

They watch TV

9. मुझको थोड़ा पानी ________________ ।

mujhko thoṛā pānī ________________ .

I want some water.

10. उसको ________________ जूता चाहिए।

usko ________________ jūtā cāhiye.

He wants a big shoe.

ANSWER KEY

A. 1. दुकान dukān 2. सड़क saṛak 3. दाएँ मुड़ो dāyẽ muṛo 4. पीछे pīche 5. चाहिए cāhiye 6. शाकाहारी śākāhārī 7. जल्दी jaldī 8. महंगा mahangā 9. कमीज़ kamīz 10. छुट्टी chuṭṭī

B. 1. मोड़ पर moṛ par 2. स्कूल के आगे skūl ke āge 3. होटल तक hotal tak 4. नदी पर nadī par 5. सड़क से saṛak se 6. शहर में śahar mẽ 7. डाकघर से dākghar se 8. पुल के पास pul ke pās 9. डाकघर के पीछे dākghar ke pīche 10. उधर तक udhar tak

C. 1. e; 2. g; 3. i; 4. j; 5. h; 6. c; 7. a; 8. b; 9. f; 10. d

D. 1. ज़्यादा zyādā 2. तैरते tairte 3. हमेशा hameśā 4. तारीख tārīkh 5. सात बजे sāt baje 6. डेढ़ बजे deṛh baje 7. बड़ा टेबल baṛā tebal 8. देखते dekhte 9. चाहिए cāhiye 10. बड़ा baṛā

How Did You Do?

Give yourself a point for every correct answer, then use the following key to determine whether or not you're ready to move on:

0–20 points: It's probably best to go back and study the lessons again to make sure you undersood everything completely. Take your time; it's not a race! Make sure you spend time reviewing the vocabulary and reading through each Grammar Builder section carefully.

20–35 points: You would benefit from a review before moving on. Go back and spend a little more time on the specific points that gave you trouble. Reread the Grammar Builder sections that were difficult and do the work outs one more time. Don't forget about the online practice material! Go to **www.livinglanguage.com/languagelab** to reinforce the material from these lessons.

35–40 points: Feel free to move on to the Review Dialogues! Great job completing the lessons in Essential Hindi.

points

Review Dialogues

Dialogue 1

Dialogue 1

Anil's maternal uncle comes visiting.

अनिल: नमस्ते मामाजी।
anil: **Namaste māmājī.**
Anil: *Hello Uncle.*

मामा: कैसे हो अनिल?
māmā: **kaise ho anil?**
Uncle: *How are you, Anil?*

अनिल: मैं मज़े में हूँ। बैठिए। क्या आपको पानी चाहिए?
anil: **maĩ maze mẽ hũ. baiṭhiye. kyā āpko pānī cāhiye?**
Anil: *I am fine. Please sit. Would you like some water?*

मामा: नहीं, चलेगा। क्या तुम्हारे माता-पिता घर पर नहीं हैं?
māmā: **nahī̃, calegā. kyā tumhāre mātā-pitā ghar par nahī̃ haĩ?**
Uncle: *No, it's okay (it will do). Aren't your parents at home?*

अनिल: जी नहीं, वे किसी काम से सुबह से बाहर हैं।
anil: **jī nahī̃, ve kisī kām se subah se bāhar haĩ.**
Anil: *No, they're out since the morning for some work.*

मामा: अच्छा। कोई नहीं। तुम कैसे हो? तुम कभी घर आओ।
māmā: acchā. koī nahī̃. tum kaise ho? tum kabhī ghar āo.
Uncle: *Oh. Okay, no problem. How are you? You should come visit us sometime.*

अनिल: जी, बिलकुल। मामीजी कैसी हैं?
anil: jī bilkul. māmījī kaisī haĩ?
Anil: *Yes, absolutely. How is Aunt?*

मामा: वह ठीक है, उसकी नई नौकरी है।
māmā: vah ṭhīk hai. uskī nayī naukri hai.
Uncle: *She is fine. She has a new job.*

अनिल: अच्छा? क्या नया ऑफिस घर के पास है?
anil: accā? kyā nayā aufis ghar ke pās hai?
Anil: *Really? Is the new office close to home?*

मामा: हाँ, नया ऑफिस पास है। वह पैदल आती-जाती है।
māmā: hā̃, nayā aufis pās hai. vah paidal ātī-jātī hai.
Uncle: *Yes, the new office is close by. She walks there and back.*

अनिल: यह तो बड़ी अच्छी बात है। लीजिए, चाय। यह समोसा भी लीजिए।
anil: yah to baṛī acchī bāt hai. lījiye, cāy. yah samosā bhī lījiye.
Anil: *This is a very good thing. Please have some tea (lit.: please take tea). Please take this samosa as well.*

मामा: वाह, समोसा बहुत अच्छा है।
māmā: vāh, samosā bahut acchā hai.
Uncle: *Wow, the samosa is very good.*

अनिल: मामाजी, एक अच्छी खबर है। देखिए, मेरी गाड़ी नई है। यह लीजिए, लड्डू।
anil: **māmājī, ek acchī khabar hai. dekhiye, merī gāṛī nayī hai. yah lījiye, laddū.**
Anil: *Uncle, there's some good news. Look, my car is a new one. Here, please take this laddu.*

मामा: अरे वाह! बधाई हो।
māmā: **arre vāh! badhāī ho.**
Uncle: *That's really good! Congratulations.*

Take It Further

Did you notice the term बैठिए **baiṭhiye** *(please sit)*? It is a form of the verb बैठना **baiṭhnā** (*to sit*). Do you remember the imperatives लो **lo** (*take*) and दो **do** (*give*) you learnt? These are mostly used when addressing in an informal manner. However, most verbs take the ending -इए **–iye** when used for addressing a person senior in age or authority. Let's take a quick look at some of these constructions, together with the imperative.

VERB (INFINITIVE FORM)	IMPERATIVE	POLITE FORM
लेना **lenā** *to take*	लो **lo**	लीजिए **lījiye**
देना **denā** *to give*	दो **do**	दीजिए **dījiye**

देखना **dekhnā** *to see*	देखो **dekho**	देखिए **dekhiye**
खाना **khānā** *to eat*	खाओ **khāo**	खाइए **khāiye**
बैठना **baiṭhnā** *to sit*	बैठो **baiṭho**	बैठिए **baiṭhiye**
करना **karnā** *to do*	करो **karo**	करिए **kariye**
आना **ānā** *to come*	आओ **āo**	आइए **āiye**

You will see more of these forms in the following dialogues.

✎ Dialogue 1 Practice

Answer the following questions based on the dialogue above.

1. मामी का नया ऑफिस किधर है?

   māmī kā nayā aufis kidhar hai?

   Where is Aunt's new office?

   ---

2. अनिल ने मामाजी को खाने के लिए क्या दिया?

   anil ne māmājī ko khāne-pīne ke liye kyā diya?

   What does Anil offer Uncle to eat and drink?

   ---

3. अनिल ने मामाजी को क्या खबर दी?

   anil ne māmājī ko kyā khabar dī?

   What news did Anil give to Uncle?

   ---

4. खबर सुन के मामाजी ने क्या कहा?

   khabar sun ke māmājī ne kyā kahā?

   What did Uncle say upon hearing the news?

   ---

5. अनिल के माता-पिता किधर हैं?

   anil ke mātā-pitā kidhar hain?

   Where are Anil's parents?

ANSWER KEY

1. मामी का नया ऑफिस घर के पास है। māmī kā nayā aufis ghar ke pās hai. *(Aunt's new office is near home.)* **2.** अनिल ने मामाजी को खाने के लिए समोसा दिया और पीने के लिए चाय दी। anil ne māmājī ko khāne ke liye samosā diya aur pīne ke liye cay dī. *(Anil gave Uncle [a] samosa to eat and tea to drink.)* **3.** अनिल ने मामाजी को यह खबर दी की उसकी नई गाड़ी है। anil ne māmājī ko yah khabar dī ki uskī nayī gaṛī hai. **4.** खबर मामाजी ने अनिल से कहा, "बधाई!" khabar sun ke māmājī ne Anil se kaha, "badhāī!" *(On hearing the news, Uncle said to Anil, "Congratulations!")* **5.** अनिल के माता-पिता किसी काम से बाहर हैं। anil ke mātā-pitā kisī kām se bāhar haĩ. (Anil's parents are out running errands/out taking care of some work.)

Dialogue 2

Dialogue 2

Vikas joins a new workplace. His colleague Seema shows him around.

सीमा: विकास, नई कंपनी में आपका स्वागत है।
sīmā: vikās, nayī kampanī mẽ āpkā swāgat hai.
Seema: *Vikas, welcome to the new company.*

विकास: धन्यवाद! मुझे भी ख़ुशी है।
vikās: dhanyavād! mujhe bhī khuśī hai.
Vikas: *Thank you! I am very happy.*

सीमा: आपका विभाग इधर है। आइए, मैं दिखाती हूँ।
sīmā: āpkā vibhāg idhar hai. āiye, maĩ dikhātī hū̃.
Seema: *Your department is over here. Please come, I will show you.*

विकास: यह ऑफिस तो बहुत बड़ा है।
vikās: yah aufis to bahut baṛā hai.
Vikas: *This office is quite big.*

सीमा: जी हाँ। यहाँ पांच सौ लोग हैं।
sīmā: **jī hā̃. yahā̃ pā̃c sau log haĩ.**
Seema: *Yes, there are five hundred people here.*

विकास: अच्छा? यह इमारत नई है। जगह बहुत सुन्दर है।
vikās: **acchā? yah īmārat nayī hai. jagah bahut sundar hai.**
Vikas: *Really? This building is new. The place is very beautiful.*

सीमा: इधर का माहौल अच्छा है, खूब सारे पेड़ हैं और खाने-पीने के लिए एक साफ़-सुथरी कैंटीन है। फलों का एक बगीचा भी है।
sīmā: **idhar kā mahaul acchā hai, khūb sāre peṛ haĩ aur khāne pīne ke liye ek sāf suthra kaintīn hai. phalõ kā ek bagīcā bhī hai.**
Seema: *The atmosphere here is very nice, there are lots of trees and a clean cafeteria as well. There is also a fruit garden.*

विकास: बहुत से पेड़ और बगीचा! यह जानकर ख़ुशी हुई। कुछ नया है।
vikās: **bahut se peṛ aur bagīcā! yah jānkar khuśī huī. kuch nayā hai.**
Vikas: *Lots of trees and a garden! Glad to hear that. This is something new.*

सीमा: और यह आपका विभाग है। यह आपकी कुर्सी है। नई जगह कैसी लगी?
sīmā: **aur yah āpkā vibhāg hai. yah āpkī kursī hai. nayī jagah kaisī lagī?**
Seema: *And this is your department. This is your chair. How do you like the new place?*

विकास: धन्यवाद! मुझे यहाँ काम करने में ख़ुशी है।
vikās: **dhanyavād! mujhe yahā̃ kām karne mẽ khuśī hai.**
Vikas: *Thank you! I am happy to work here (to do work here).*

Take It Further

Did you notice two new words? ऑफिस **aufis** (*office*) is an English loanword. There are two Hindi words for *office*. These are दफ्तर **daphtar** and कार्यालय **kāryālay**. However, these days, ऑफिस **aufis** is the most commonly-used one.

The common word for *cafeteria* in Hindi is also a loanword, **Canteen**. The Hindi way literally means खाने की जगह **khāne kī jagah** (*place for food/to eat and drink*) or नाश्ते की जगह **naśte kī jagah** (*place for snacks*).

Dialogue Practice 2

1. सीमा विकास को क्या दिखाती है?

   sīmā vikās ko kyā dikhatī hai?

   What does Seema show Vikas?

   ___

2. विकास के नए ऑफिस में कितने लोग हैं?

   vikās ke naye aufis mẽ kitne log haĩ?

   How many people work in Vikas's office? (lit.: how many people are there in Vikas's office?)

   ___

3. क्या विकास का नया ऑफिस बड़ा है?

   kyā vikās kā nayā aufis baṛā hai?

   Is Vikas's new office large?

   ___

4. विकास ने सीमा से ऑफिस के बारे में क्या कहा?

vikās ne sīmā se aufis ke bāre mẽ kyā kahā?

What did Vikas tell Seema about the Office?

---

5. क्या ऑफिस में कैंटीन है?

kyā aufis mẽ kainteen hai?

Is there a cafeteria in the office?

ANSWER KEY

1. सीमा विकास को नया विभाग दिखाती है। **sīmā vikās ko nayā vibhāg dikhātī hai.** (*Seema shows Vikas the new department.*) 2. नए ऑफिस में 500 लोग हैं। **naye aufis mẽ 500 log haĩ.** (*There are 500 people in the new office.*) 3. हाँ, विकास का नया ऑफिस बड़ा है। **hā̃, vikās kā nayā aufis baṛā hai.** (*Yes, Vikas's new office is large.*) 4. विकास ने सीमा से कहा कि इमारत नई है और जगह बहुत सुन्दर है। **vikās ne sīmā se kaha ki īmārat nayī hai aur jagah bahut sundar hai.** (*Vikas said to Seema that the building is new and the place is very beautiful.*) 5. हाँ, ऑफिस में एक साफ़ सुथरी कैंटीन है। **hā̃, aufis mẽ ek sā̃f suthrī kaintīn hai.** (*Yes, there is a clean cafeteria in the office.*)

Dialogue 3

Dialogue 3

Zoya goes shopping.

ज़ोया: भैया, कोई हरी सब्ज़ी है?
zoyā: bhaiyā, koī harī sabzī hai?
Zoya: Sir (lit.: brother), do you have any green vegetables?

दूकानदार: जी हाँ, पालक है।
dukāndār: jī hā̃, pālak hai.
Storekeeper: Yes (ma'am), I have (lit.: there is) spinach.

ज़ोया: ज़रा दिखाओ।
zoyā: zarā dikhāo.
Zoya: Show me some.

दूकानदार: यह देखिये। एकदम ताज़ी हैं।
dukāndār: yah dekhiye. ekdam tāzī hai.
Storekeeper: Please take a look (lit.: see). (It's) very fresh.

ज़ोया: क्या दाम है?
zoyā: kyā dām hai?
Zoya: How much is it? (lit.: What's the price?)

दूकानदार: ४० रुपये की एक किलो।
dukāndār: cālīs rupye kī ek kilo.
Storekeeper: Forty rupees per kilo.

ज़ोया: यह तो महँगी है।
zoyā: yah to mahangī hai.
Zoya: It's expensive.

दूकानदार: नहीं बहनजी, आप आगे पूछ लीजिये, यही दाम है।
dukāndār: nahī̃ bahanji, āp āge pūch lījiye, yahī dām hai.
Storekeeper: No, Ma'am (lit.: sister), you can ask elsewhere (lit.: ahead), this is the price.

ज़ोया: अच्छा ठीक है। खीरा और टमाटर हैं?
zoyā: acchā ṭhīk hai. khīrā aur tamātar haĩ?
Zoya: Ok, fine. Do you have cucumbers and tomatoes?

दुकानदार: टमाटर नहीं हैं। लेकिन खीरा है।
dukāndār: tamātar nahī̃ haĩ. lekin khīrā hai.
Storekeeper: There are no tomatoes. But there's cucumber.

ज़ोया: क्या दाम है?
zoyā: kyā dām hai?
Zoya: How much is it? (lit.: What's the price?)

दुकानदार: २० रूपये का ५०० ग्राम।
dukāndār: bīs rupye kā pā̃c sau grām.
Storekeeper: 20 rupees for 500 grams.

ज़ोया: मुझे २५० ग्राम देना।
zoyā: mujhe 250 grām denā.
Zoya: Give me 250 grams.

Take It Further

In Hindi, unknown people often address each other as भैया **bhaiyā** (*elder brother*), बहन **bahan** (*sister*), भाभी **bhābhī** (*brother's wife*), or चाचा **cācā** (*uncle*), depending on the age.

Dialogue Practice 3

1. ज़ोया किधर है?

   zoyā kidhar hai?

   Where is Zoya?

2. ज़ोया को क्या चाहिए?

zoyā ko kyā cāhiye?

What does Zoya want (to buy)?

3. ज़ोया को और क्या चाहिए?

zoyā ko aur kyā cāhiye?

What else does Zoya want?

4. हरी सब्ज़ी का क्या दाम है?

harī sabzī kā kyā dām hai?

How much do the green vegetables cost? (lit.: What's the price of green vegetables?)

5. टमाटर का क्या दाम है?

tamātar kā kyā dām hai?

How much do the tomatoes cost?

ANSWER KEY

1. ज़ोया बाज़ार में है। **zoyā bāzār mẽ hai.** (*Zoya is in the market.*) 2. ज़ोया को हरी सब्ज़ी चाहिए। **zoyā ko harī sabzī cāhiye.** (*Zoya wants green vegetables.*) 3. ज़ोया को टमाटर और खीरा चाहिए। **zoyā ko ṭamāṭar aur khīrā cāhiye.** (*Zoya wants cucumbers and tomatoes.*) 4. हरी सब्ज़ी ४० रुपये किलो है। **harī sabzī pacās rupye kilo hai.** (*The green vegetables cost fifty rupees a kilo.*) 5. टमाटर २० रूपये के ५०० ग्राम हैं। **ṭamāṭar bīs rupye ke pāc sau grām haĩ.** (*The tomatoes cost 20 Rupees for 500 grams.*)

Dialogue 4

Dialogue 4

Meeta meets an old friend at the college she has just joined.

मीता: अरे नैना, तुम यहाँ?
mītā: **are nainā, tum yahā̃?**
Meeta: *Hello, Naina! What are you doing here?*

नैना: कैसी हो मीता? मैं यहाँ पढ़ती हूँ।
nainā: **kaisī ho mītā? maĩ yahā̃ paṛhtī hū̃.**
Naina: *How are you, Meeta? I study here.*

मीता: तुम कौनसी कक्षा में हो?
mītā: **tum kaunsī kakśā mẽ ho?**
Meeta: *Which class are you in?*

नैना: गणित की कक्षा में। और तुम?
nainā: **gaṇit kī kakśā mẽ. aur tum?**
Naina: *In the Math class. And you?*

मीता: मैं भी गणित की कक्षा में ही हूँ। तुम कालेज के बाद क्या करती हो?
mītā: **maĩ bhī gaṇit kī kakśā mẽ hī hū̃. tum kālej ke bād kyā kartī ho?**
Meeta: *I too am in the Math class. What do you do after college?*

नैना: मैं और कुछ लोग मिलकर शाम को बच्चों को पढ़ाते हैं।
nainā: **maĩ aur kuch log milkar śām ko baccõ ko paṛhāte haĩ.**
Naina: *Some other people and I teach children together in the evening.*

मीता:	अच्छा? कौनसे बच्चे?
mītā:	**acchā? kaun se bacce?**
Meeta:	*Really? Which children?*
नैना:	मेरी कालोनी के कुछ गरीब बच्चे हैं।
nainā:	**merī kālonī ke kuch garīb bacce haĩ.**
Naina:	*Some poor children from my area (colony).*
मीता:	यह तो बहुत अच्छा काम है। चलो, आज से मैं भी आती हूँ।
mītā:	**yah to bahut acchā kām hai. calo, āj se maĩ bhī ātī hū̃.**
Meeta:	*This is a very good thing (work). Come on, I'm coming too.*
नैना:	बिलकुल! यह तो और भी अच्छी बात है। हमको मदद चाहिए।
nainā:	**bilkul! yah to aur bhī acchī bāt hai. hamko madad cāhiye**
Naina:	*Absolutely! This is even better. We need help.*

Dialogue Practice

1. नैना कहाँ पढ़ती है?

   nainā kahā̃ paṛhtī hai?

   Where does Naina study?

2. मीता और नैना किधर मिलते हैं?

   mītā aur nainā kidhar milte haĩ?

   Where do Meeta and Naina meet?

3. नैना कौनसी कक्षा में हैं?

nainā kaunsī kakśā mẽ haĩ?

Which class are Meeta and Naina in?

---

4. नैना शाम को क्या करती है?

nainā śhām ko kyā kartī hai?

What does Naina do in the evening?

---

5. नैना किसको पढ़ाती है?

nainā kisko paṛhātī hai?

Who does Naina teach?

ANSWER KEY

1. नैना कालेज में पढ़ती है। **nainā kālej mẽ paṛhtī hai.** (*Naina studies at the college.*) 2. मीता और नैना कालेज में मिलते हैं। **mītā aur nainā kālej mẽ milte haĩ.** (*Meeta and Naina meet at the college.*) 3. नैना गणित की कक्षा में है। **nainā gaṇit kī kakśā mẽ hai.** (*Naina is in the Math class.*) 4. नैना शाम को बच्चों को पढ़ाती है। **nainā śhām ko baccõ ko paṛhātī hai.** (*Naina teaches children in the evening.*) 5. नैना कालोनी के गरीब बच्चों को पढ़ाती है। **nainā kāloni ke garīb baccõ ko paṛhātī hai.** (*Naina teaches some poor children of her area.*)

Dialogue 5

Dialogue 5

Ganesh answers the phone.

गणेश: हैलो?

gaṇesh: hailo?

Ganesh: Hello?

अजय: हैलो, कौन, गणेश? मैं अजय हूं।
ajay: **helo, kaun, gaṇesh? mai ajay hū̃.**
Ajay: *Hello, is this (lit.: who) Ganesh? This is Ajay (speaking).*

गणेश: कैसे हो, अजय?
gaṇesh: **kaise ho ajay?**
Ganesh: *How are you, Ajay?*

अजय: मैं मज़े में हूं। आप बोलो। बहुत व्यस्त रहते हैं आजकल।
ajay: **maĩ maze me hū̃. āp bolo. bahut vyast rahte haĩ ājkal.**
Ajay: *I'm fine. How about you? (lit.: You say something about yourself.) You're very busy these days.*

गणेश: हाँ, लेकिन अभी गरमी की छुट्टी है और मुझको घर पर आराम करना पसंद है।
gaṇesh: **hā̃. lekin abhī garmī kī chuṭṭī hai aur mujhko ghar par ārām karnā pasand hai.**
Ganesh: *Yes. But right now it's the summer holidays and I like to rest at home.*

अजय: ओह। क्या आपको क्रिकेट खेलना पसंद है? मैं और मेरे मित्र रोज़ खेलते हैं। आप भी चलो।
ajay: **oh. kyā āpko kriket khelnā pasand hai? maĩ aur mere mitra roz khelte haĩ. āp bhī calo.**
Ajay: *Oh. Do you like to play cricket? My friends and I play every day. You can join us, too. (lit.: you come with us as well.)*

गणेश: हाँ बिलकुल। तुम सब कब और किधर खेलते हो?
gaṇesh: **hā̃ bilkul! tum sab kab aur kidhar khelte ho?**
Ganesh: *Yes, sure! When and where do you all play?*

अजय:	हम शाम साढ़े सात बजे, अम्बर नगर के मैदान में खेलते हैं।
ajay:	**ham śhām sāṛhe sāt baje, ambar nagar ke maidan mẽ khelte haĩ.**
Ajay:	*We play in the evening at 7:30 pm, at the Ambar Nagar (colony) ground.*
गणेश:	बहुत अच्छे। तो कल मिलते हैं।
gaṇesh:	**bahut acche! to kal milte haĩ.**
Ganesh:	*Very good! So (then) we'll meet tomorrow.*
अजय:	अच्छा, मिलते हैं।
ajay:	**acchā, milte haĩ.**
Ajay:	*Okay (fine), see you (we'll meet then).*

Dialogue Practice

1. गणेश फोन पर किसके साथ बात करता है?

   gaṇesh fon par kiske sāth bāt kartā hai?

   Who is Ganesh talking to on the phone?

2. गणेश को गर्मी की छुट्टियों में क्या पसंद है?

   gaṇesh ko garmī kī chuṭṭiyõ mẽ kyā pasand hai?

   What does Ganesh like to do in summer holidays?

3. अजय और उसके मित्र क्या खेलते हैं?

   ajay aur uske mitra kyā khelte haĩ?

   Where do Ajay and his friends play?

4. क्या गणेश को क्रिकेट पसंद है?

kyā gaṇesh ko kriket pasand hai?

Does Ganesh like cricket?

ANSWER KEY

1. गणेश अजय के साथ बात करता है। **gaṇesh ajay ke sāth bāt kartā hai.** (*Ganesh is talking to Ajay.*) 2. गणेश को गर्मी की छुट्टियों में आराम करना पसंद है। **gaṇesh ko garmī kī chuṭṭiyõ mẽ ārām karnā pasand hai.** (*Ganesh likes to rest up during summer holidays.*) 3. अजय और उसके मित्र क्रिकेट खेलते हैं। **ajay aur uske mitra kriket khelte haĩ.** (*Ajay and his friends play cricket.*) 4. हाँ, गणेश को क्रिकेट पसंद है। **hã, gaṇesh ko kriket pasand hai.** (*Yes, Ganesh likes cricket.*)

Devanagari and Hindi Pronunciation

Hindi is written in a script called Devanagari. This beautiful script is actually much easier to learn than you might think, and once you learn it, you can pronounce any Hindi word you see. That is because with few exceptions, Hindi, unlike English, is phonetic. But before introducing individual letters and their pronunciation, it's important to take note of a few concepts about Hindi and Devanagari.

First, Devanagari is, in technical terms, a syllabary rather than an alphabet. This means that each Devanagari letter represents a syllable, most of which consist of a consonant followed by a vowel, something like "duh" or "guh." In fact, the vowel sound in these examples—which is similar to the sound at the ends of the words *soda* or *yoga*—is inherently pronounced along with each Devanagari consonant. It's as if whenever you see "d" or "g" you automatically pronounce "duh" or "guh," respectively. But Hindi has other vowels, and they're written either as hooks or similar marks above or below the consonant, or as separate letters, either before or after the consonant. The following are a few simple examples that demonstrate this:

क	This is the basic letter pronounced like the "k" in *kite*. But it also has the inherent vowel, so it's pronounced "kuh." In the standard transliteration used for Hindi, it's written ka. Make sure you pronounce this a like the "a" in *soda* or *yoga*, and not like the vowels in *cat* or *hot*.

के	This is the letter "k" with the short vowel "eh," as in *bet*. Notice that it's a kind of slash or hook above the letter. So this is pronounced **ke.**
की	Here we have "k" with the vowel "ee," as in *see*. This is pronounced like *key*, and in transliteration it's **kī**. Notice that **ī** comes after its host consonant.
कि	And here we have an example of a vowel that comes before its host consonant. It's the shorter "ih," as in *his*. So this is pronounced **ki**.

Vowels in Hindi can also occur independently of a consonant, for example, if a word begins with a vowel or when a vowel comes after another vowel. Therefore, Hindi has two forms of each vowel. Here are examples of the four vowels you just saw, this time at the beginning of the words, so in independent forms:

अक **ak**	ईक **īk**
एक **ek**	इक **ik**

And here are two examples of a vowel coming after another vowel. Notice that the first vowel is written above the host consonant, and the second vowel takes its independent form.

केआ **keā**	केऊ **keū**

Again, remember that अक **ak** is pronounced like the last part of "stuck" and not "stack." Also notice that the independent forms of vowels don't necessarily look like the hosted forms. You just have to memorize them. But if it's any consolation, there is no distinction in Devanagari between upper- and lowercase letters, so you only need to learn one form of the consonants. Finally, you can see that most Devanagari letters are formed with a headstroke—a horizontal line—and that the rest of the letter appears to dangle beneath it. A few of the independent vowels break this line, such as अक **ak**, and many of the hosted vowels are written above it, as in the case of ईक **īk**. We'll come back to this in a moment.

Now let's look at two very important features of Hindi pronunciation. If you've ever heard an Indian person speaking English, you may have noticed a unique quality of their consonants. For example, a "t" or a "d" may sound as if it's pronounced with the tongue further back in the mouth, almost curled backward. This is because Hindi distinguishes between dental consonants—ones that are pronounced with the tongue placed against the teeth—and retroflex consonants—ones that are pronounced with the tongue curled up against the roof of the mouth. So, there are separate Devanagari letters for dental **t** and retroflex **ṭ**. Note the small dot in transliteration; this is how retroflex consonants are marked.

Hindi also distinguishes between aspirated and nonaspirated consonants. Aspirated consonants are pronounced with a puff of air, and nonaspirated consonants are pronounced almost as if the breath is being held. We have an approximation of this in English. Say the words *pool* and *spool* aloud, while holding a finger right in front of your mouth. In *pool*, there is a little puff of air with the "p" that you can feel quite noticeably on your finger. That's the aspiration. But in *spool*, the "p" has a different quality—you can hardly feel any air on your finger when you say it. In English, this quality is just something that happens because of neighboring sounds. English speakers hardly notice it and certainly don't distinguish words by whether a sound is aspirated or not. But in Hindi this distinction is the basis for two entirely different consonants, and words differ just based on whether a particular consonant is aspirated or not. In transliteration the aspirated consonants are written with an **h**. But don't pronounce it as a separate letter. It's just there to mark the aspirated consonants, like the dot does in retroflex consonants.

With these distinctions, you have four forms of "t" in Hindi: t, ṭ, th, and ṭh.

t – dental, nonaspirated	th – dental, aspirated
ṭ – retroflex, nonaspirated	ṭh – retroflex, aspirated

The challenge for English speakers is that our consonants tend to be "mushy" mixtures of these fine distinctions, halfway between aspirated and nonaspirated, and halfway between dental and retroflex. But don't worry; with a little practice, it's not that difficult. We'll get into the quality of each consonant in more detail in a moment. First, let's start with the vowels.

Vowels

Hindi has eleven vowel sounds. Remember that there are two forms of each vowel in Devanagari—an independent form, which you use if a word starts with a vowel, and a hosted form, which you write above, below, before, or after the host consonant. You'll see each vowel in both forms, independent, and then hosted on the letter क, or k.

अ		क	a, ka. This is the neutral vowel in the English words *soda*, *photography*, or *parameter*. Remember that every Devanagari letter that isn't marked with a vowel is pronounced with this "inherent" vowel. The exception is the final consonant of a word; that's usually pronounced without the inherent vowel.

आ	ा	का	ā, kā. This is a longer vowel, like in the English *car* or *dark*.
इ	ि	कि	i, ki. This vowel is like the short "ih" in *his* or *pit*.
ई	ी	की	ī, kī. This is the longer "ee" sound of *see* or *dream*. But be careful to make it a crisp sound, not drawn out like the English "ee-yuh."
उ	ु	कु	u, ku. This vowel is like the "uh" of *pull* or *foot*.
ऊ	ू	कू	ū, kū. This is the longer "oo" of *pool* or *fool*. But don't draw it out with the "w" sound heard in English.
ऋ	ृ	कृ	ṛ, kṛ. This is an "r," but it's a vowel rather than a consonant. It's similar to the "rih" of *written* or *riddle*.
ए	े	के	e, ke. This is a very short, crisp and pure sound, like a clipped "ay" of *same* or *lake*. If you pronounce the English words very slowly, you'll hear that there's a lot of "ee" in that "ay." Try to cut the sound off before you get to the "ee," and you'll have the Hindi sound. If you speak French or Spanish, it's like *parlé* or *sabe*.
ऐ	ै	कै	ai, kai. This is like the short "eh" of English *get* or *carry*.
ओ	ो	को	o, ko. This is another short, crisp and pure sound, similar to the beginning of the "oh" of *sofa* or *hotel*. But again, say those words slowly, and you'll hear a lot of "oo" and "w" in English. Cut those parts out, and you'll have the Hindi. If you speak French or Spanish, it's like the sound in *hôtel* or *pone*.
औ	ौ	कौ	au, kau. This is either the sound in *auto* or *gown*.

NASALIZED VOWELS

Any vowel, with the exception of ṛ, can be nasalized. That means that a good part of the airflow passes through the nose. You may not realize it, but English has plenty of nasal vowels. Any time a vowel comes before –m, –n, or –ng in the same syllable, it's nasalized. Say *dope* and *don't*, and pay close attention to the vowel. It's nasalized in *don't*. In Hindi, a nasal vowel is marked by a kind of half-moon on its side with a dot over it, placed above the vowel. If part of the vowel itself is written above the headstroke, then just the dot is used. Notice that in transliteration, nasalization is marked by the tilde:

कूँ **kū̃**, काँ **kā̃**, कों **kõ**.

Let's look at nasalization of the vowels and nasalization on the consonant क.

अ, अं*	क, कं	**a, ã, ka, kã**
आ, आं	का, कां	**ā, ā̃, kā, kā̃**
इ, इं	कि, किं	**i, ĩ, ki, kĩ**
ई, ईं	की, कीं	**ī, ī̃, kī, kī̃**
उ, उं	कु, कुं	**u, ũ, ku, kũ**
ऊ, ऊं	कू, कूं	**ū, ū̃, kū, kū̃**
ऋ,ऋं	कृ, कृं	**ṛ, ṛī̃ kṛ, kṛī̃**
ए, एं	के, कें	**e, ẽ, ke, kẽ**
ऐ, ऐं	कै, कैं	**ai, aĩ, kai, kaĩ**

ओ, ओं	को, कों	o, õ, ko, kõ
औ, औं	कौ, कौं	au, aũ, kau, kaũ
**In this table, only the dots are used above the nasal vowels. You'll see the full appearance of nasal vowels—with the half moon and dot—later in this book.*		

Note that केक **kek** (*cake*) and कुक **kuk** (*cook*) have been incorporated into the language in their original forms. Hindi, like most languages, has many such loanwords that it has borrowed from other languages, including English.

क ka, ख kha, ग ga, and घ gha

Now let's look at the Hindi consonants. We're going to present them in an order that will make it easier for you to understand how they're pronounced. It's not the normal order of Devanagari, as you'd use in a dictionary. You'll learn that later. Remember that each of these Devanagari letters automatically includes the inherent "a" vowel.

These four consonants are called "velar" consonants, because they're made with your tongue against the "velum," which is just a technical term meaning the back part of the roof of your mouth, also called the "soft palate."

क	**ka**. This is the consonant in *skit* or *school*, without any puff of air. Try to say those words while holding your breath, imagining that there's a match in front of your mouth that you don't want to blow out!
ख	**kha**. And this is the aspirated form, similar to the consonant in *kit* or *cool*. This time, try to blow out that match when you say it!

ग	ga. This is an non-aspirated "g," similar to the consonant in *angry* or *gleam*. Again, there shouldn't be any puff of air. Try to say "go" while holding your breath. Hold your fingers right in front of your mouth, and if you feel a puff of air, keep trying!
घ	gha. This is the aspirated form of "g." Say *go* or *get*, holding your fingers in front of your mouth, and try to release a puff of air as you say the "g."

च ca, छ cha, ज ja, झ jha

These four sounds are called "palatal" because you use your palate, or the roof of your mouth, to pronounce them. Say "gob" and "job," and you'll feel your tongue slide forward from the velar "g" to the palatal "j."

च	ca. This is similar to the sound in *cheese* or *cheat*, but without any puff of air. The other major difference is that the tongue is behind the lower teeth, rather than the upper teeth. That will arch the tongue up against the palate.
छ	cha. And this is the aspirated form of ca. Say *choose* or *church*, with your tongue behind the lower teeth, and try to blow out that match.
ज	ja. This is similar to the sound in *jeep* or *jeer*, but again, with the tongue behind the lower teeth, the tongue arched against the roof of the mouth, and no puff of air.
झ	jha. This is the aspirated form of ja.

त ta, थ tha, द da, ध dha

Now let's look at the dental sounds. They're similar to English consonants, but the tongue is against the back of the upper teeth.

त	ta. Say the "t" in *tea* or *time*, but move your tongue a bit forward. In English, you use the little ridge behind the upper teeth. In Hindi, you use the teeth themselves. Also, since this is non-aspirated, you won't produce a puff of air.
थ	tha. This is the aspirated form of t. Keep everything the same as above, but this time make a puff of air.
द	da. This is like the "d" in *dream* or *drew*, but again, pronounced with the tongue against the upper teeth, and without any puff of air.
ध	dha. This is the aspirated form of da.

ट ṭa, ठ ṭha, ड ḍa, ढ ḍha

Now let's focus on the retroflex consonants. These are all pronounced with the tongue curled backwards, away from the teeth. If the dental consonants are pronounced "further up" than their English counterparts, the retroflex are pronounced "further back."

ट	ṭa. Say the English *try* or *trim*, and notice that your tongue is further back than when you say *tie* or *Tim*. The Hindi retroflex is just a little bit further back still. And since this is non-aspirated, be careful not to produce a puff of air as you say it.
ठ	ṭha. This is the aspirated form of ṭa

ड	ḍa. Say the English *dream* or *drum*, and then slide your tongue back a bit further. Be careful to say this without any aspiration.
ढ	ḍha. This is the aspirated form of ḍa.

प pa, फ pha, ब ba, भ bha

These consonants are all formed with the lips, which is why they are called "labials."

प	pa. This consonant is similar to the "p" in *spool* or *spin*, said with no aspiration at all, meaning no puff of air. If you were to say it in front of a candle, the candle would stay lit.
फ	pha. This is the aspirated form of pa. It's closer to the "p" in *pool* or *pin*, but with more of a puff of air.
ब	ba. This is like the b in *bit* or *bin*, but with no puff of air.
भ	bha. This is the aspirated form of ba.

ङ ṅa, ञ ña, ण ṇa, न na, म ma

Now let's look at the nasal consonants. As you can guess, they're called nasals because they're pronounced—at least partially—through the nose.

ङ	ṅa. Don't be intimidated by the strange dot on the "n." You pronounce this consonant whenever you say *sing* or *ink*. Technically, this is a velar nasal—you make it with your tongue in the same position as "k" or "g."

ञ	ña. This is the palatal n sound, which is just like the "ny" in *onion* or *canyon*. If you know any Spanish, the transliteration will look familiar.
ण	ṇa. As you can guess from the dot below the letter, this is a retroflex version of n. Say *no* or *need* with the tongue curled back in the mouth, behind where you say "ny."
न	na. This is a dental n, probably the closest variety to the English *no* or *need*, but the tongue is placed against the upper teeth, rather than against the ridge just behind the teeth.
म	ma. And this is not an "n" at all, but rather the "m" sound of *mom* or *make*. Notice that it's still a nasal sound, which is why it's grouped here.

श śa, ष ṣa, स sa, र ra, ड़ ṛa, ढ़ ṛha

The consonants in this group are all related to the letter "s" and "r." in English.

श	śa. This is the "sh" sound in *ship* or *shoe*.
ष	ṣa. This is technically a retroflex version of śa, so it would be pronounced with the tongue further back in the mouth. But it's usually not distinguished from śa in normal speech.
स	sa. This is like the "s" is *see* or *same*.
र	ra. This is a rolled r, like the Spanish *perro*, but shorter.
ड़	ṛa. This is a retroflex ra sound, produced with the tongue further back in the mouth.
ढ़	ṛha. This is the aspirated version of ṛa.

ह ha, य ya, व va, ल la, ज़ za

The consonants in this group are a bit of a mixed bag.

ह	ha. This is the consonant in *have* or *head*.
य	ya. This is the consonant in *year* and *yes*.
व	va. This is a sound similar to the "v" in *very* or *vat*, but the lower lip doesn't come into contact with the upper teeth, so it has a bit of a "w" sound to it.
ल	la. This is the "l" of *long* and *life*, but the tongue is pushed against the upper teeth.
ज़	za. This is the sound of *zipper* or *zest*.

Grammar Summary

1. PRONOUNS

मैं	*I*
तुम	*you*
वह	*she/he/it/that*
यह	*she/he/it/this*
हम	*we*
आप	*you*
वे	*they/those*
ये	*they/those*

2. EMPHATIC PRONOUNS

अपने आप	*by oneself/self*
खुद	*by oneself/self*

3. POSSESSIVE PRONOUNS

MASCULINE SINGULAR	FEMININE SINGULAR	
मेरा	मेरी	*mine*
तुम्हारा	तुम्हारी	*your/yours*
आपका	आपकी	*your/yours*
हमारा	हमारी	*our/ours*
उसका	उसकी	*her/hers; his; of that*
इसका	इसकी	*her/hers; his; of this*

MASCULINE PLURAL	FEMININE PLURAL	
मेरे	मेरी	*my/mine*
तुम्हारे	तुम्हारी	*your/yours*
आपके	आपकी	*your/yours*
हमारे	हमारी	*our/ours*
उसके	उसकी	*her/hers; his; of that*
इसके	इसकी	*her/hers; his; of this*
उनके	उनकी	*their/theirs/of those*
इनके	इनकी	*their/theirs/of these*

4. VERB TENSES

होना (*TO BE*) — PRESENT TENSE

मैं हूँ	*I am*
तुम हो	*you are*
वह है	*she/he/it/that is*
यह है	*she/he/it/this is*
हम हैं	*we are*
आप हैं	*you are*
वे हैं	*they/those are*
ये हैं	*they/these are*

होना (*TO BE*) — PAST TENSE

	MASCULINE	FEMININE	
मैं	था	थी	*I was*
तुम	थे	थीं	*you were*
वह	था	थी	*she/he/it/that was*
यह	था	थी	*she/he/it/this was*
हम	थे	थीं	*we were*
आप	थे	थीं	*you were*
वे	थे	थीं	*they/those were*
ये	थे	थीं	*they/these were*

होना (*TO BE*) — FUTURE TENSE

	MASCULINE	FEMININE	
मैं	हूँगा	हूंगी	*I will be*
तुम	होगे	होगी	*you will be*
आप	होंगे	होंगी	*you will be*
हम	होंगे	होंगी	*we will be*
यह/वह	होगा	होगी	*he/she/it will be*
ये/वे	होंगे	होंगी	*they will be*

THE PRESENT IMPERFECTIVE

Verb stem (infinitive without –ना ending) conjugated as per gender and number + Conjugated form of होना (*to be*)

खाना (*TO EAT*) — PRESENT IMPERFECTIVE

	MASCULINE	FEMININE	
मैं	खाता हूँ	खाती हूँ	*I eat*
तुम	खाते हो	खाती हो	*you eat*
वह	खाता है	खाती है	*she/he/it/that eats*
यह	खाता है	खाती है	*she/he/it/this eats*
हम	खाते हैं	खाती हैं	*we eat*
आप	खाते हैं	खाती हैं	*you eat*

वे	खाते हैं	खाती हैं	*they/those eat*
ये	खाते हैं	खाती हैं	*they/these eat*

CONSTRUCTIONS IN CONTINUOUS TENSES

Main verb stem (without the ending –ना) + Appropriate conjugation of रहना (*to stay*) + conjugation of होना according to pronoun and tense

खाना (*TO EAT*) — PRESENT CONTINUOUS

	MASCULINE	FEMININE	
मैं	खा रहा हूँ	खा रही हूँ	*I am eating*
तुम	खा रहे हो	खा रही हो	*you are eating*
वह	खा रहा है	खा रही है	*she/he/it/that is eating*
यह	खा रहा है	खा रही है	*she/he/it/this is eating*
हम	खा रहे हैं	रही हैं	*we are eating*
आप	रहे हैं	खा रही हैं	*you are eating*
वे	खा रहे हैं	खा रही हैं	*they/those are eating*
ये	खा रहे हैं	खा रही हैं	*they/these are eating*

खाना (*TO EAT*) — PAST CONTINUOUS

	MASCULINE	FEMININE	
मैं	खा रहा था	खा रही थी	*I was eating*
तुम	खा रहे थे	खा रही थी	*you were eating*
वह	खा रहा था	खा रही थी	*she/he/it/that was eating*
यह	खा रहा था	खा रही थी	*she/he/it/this was eating*
हम	खा रहे थे	रही थीं	*we were eating*
आप	खा रहे थे	खा रही थीं	*you were eating*
वे	खा रहे थे	खा रही थीं	*they/those were eating*
ये	खा रहे थे	खा रही थीं	*they/these were eating*

खाना (*TO EAT*) — FUTURE CONTINUOUS

	MASCULINE	FEMININE	
मैं	खा रहा हूँगा	खा रही रही	*I will be eating*
तुम	खा रहे होगे	खा रही होगी	*you will be eating*
वह	खा रहा था	खा रही होगी	*she/he/it/that will be eating*
यह	खा रहा था	खा रही होगी	*she/he/it/this will be eating*

हम	खा रहे होंगे	खा रही होंगी	*we will be eating*
आप	खा रहे होंगे	खा रही होंगी	*you will be eating*
वे	खा रहे होंगे	खा रही होंगी	*they/those will be eating*
ये	खा रहे होंगे	खा रही होंगी	*they/these will be eating*

5. COMPOUND VERBS

Main verb without the ending –ना + helping verb

INFINITIVE MAIN VERB	HELPING VERB	COMPOUND VERB	
सोना	जाना	सो जाना	*to fall asleep*
भूलना	जाना	भूल जाना	*to forget completely*
करना	लेना	कर लेना	*to do*

Compound verbs add emphasis and a sense of completion of the action. By itself the verb conveys meaning, but a compound verb conveys certainty of purpose.

Compound verbs behave like other verbs and express the present, past, and future tenses and the imperative; but they do not have a continuous tense.

6. CONJUNCT VERBS

ADJECTIVE + VERB

काम करना	*to work*
सफाई करना	*to clean*
आराम करना	*to rest*

7. POSTPOSITIONS

COMMON POSTPOSITIONS

में	*in/around*
पर	*on/at*
से	*from*
तक	*up to/till*

COMPOUND POSTPOSITIONS

THE PARTICLE के (*OF/TO*) + ADJECTIVES

के पास	*near to something*
के पीछे	*behind something*
के नीचे	*under something*
के ऊपर	*above something*
के आगे	*ahead of something*

8. COMPARATIVES

अच्छा	*good*
उससे अच्छा/ज़्यादा अच्छा/और अच्छा	*better*
सबसे अच्छा	*best*

9. INTERROGATIVES

क्या	*what*
कब	*when*
कहाँ	*where*
कैसे	*how*
कौन	*who*
कितना	*how many?*

10. POLITE REQUESTS

Subject pronoun + object + conjugated form of चाहना or पसंद करना (*to like*) according to the subject

Subject pronoun + object + मिलना conjugated according to gender and number of noun

11. EXPRESSING OBLIGATION

Subject + को + object + चाहिए + appropriate form of auxiliary verb होना

EXPRESSING OBLIGATION IN THE PAST TENSE

Subject + को + object + conjugated main verb agreeing in gender and number with object + चाहिए + past tense of होना (था/थे/थी/थीं) agreeing in gender and number with object.